FAMILY POLICY IN THE USSR
SINCE 1944

BY: APRIL A. VON FRANK

PALO ALTO, CALIFORNIA
1979

PUBLISHED BY

R & E RESEARCH ASSOCIATES, INC.
936 INDUSTRIAL AVENUE
PALO ALTO, CALIFORNIA 94303

PUBLISHERS

ROBERT D. REED AND ADAM S. ETEROVICH

Library of Congress Card Catalog Number

77 1123

I.S.B.N.

0-88247-552-5

TABLE OF CONTENTS

INTRODUCTION

The following study is an examination of Soviet family policies since 1944 dealing with family allowances, abortion and contraception, divorce and illegitimacy, child care facilities and maternity benefits, and motherhood awards. I will discuss the problems of Soviet society that brought about these policies as well as how the policies were directed toward encouraging fertility and, at the same time, promoting female labor force participation in the Soviet population. In addition, I plan to examine whether or not the policies helped to promote these goals and the reasons they were or were not successful.

I have divided my discussion into four parts. The first part examines the immediate and practical problems facing the USSR after World War II when the policies were first instituted. Also included is a description of the content and subsequent changes in each policy. The second part analyzes the application of Soviet policy to the population, i.e., to which groups or areas of the country various policies were directed. This analysis is important in order to evaluate the effectiveness of family policies. If policies were not equally applicable to the same groups within the population, an examination of the general population alone would not throw much light on the intent or effects of the policies. Thus I have distinguished the family policies that apply mainly to the urban and rural populations and, where important, to European or non-European nationality groups within the urban-rural dichotomy. The reason emphasis is given to urban-rural differences is that they are the essential socio-economic and cultural differences in the USSR and are crucial in understanding family policies.

The third part of the discussion includes an evaluation of the effectiveness of Soviet policy in achieving its goals. Attention will center on the major social and economic changes occurring in the USSR since 1944 that are largely responsible for the success or lack of success of family policies. Finally, part four will relate the origin and changes in family policy to the Marxist-Leninist ideological base of Soviet society. Current debates over both ideology and policy will be included. These debates provide not only an understanding of how the Soviets explain the dynamics of their society and the effectiveness of family policies, but also how they conceive of and propose to deal with current problems.

Admittedly, it is difficult to provide any precise quantitative measurement of the success of failure of family policies, and I have not attempted this. Fertility and female employment are affected by many factors, and family policy should be considered largely as an "intervening variable." Socio-economic trends associated with modernization are the major factors in differential fertility and labor force trends, and it is against this broader background that family policies are being evaluated. Thus a more qualitative, rather than quantitative assessment of the role of family policies in fertility and female employment trends will be given. The following kinds of evidence will be employed in my discussion: trends in Soviet fertility (using such measures as birth rates and family size) and female labor force trends; Soviet research on the family dealing with family policy, fertility, and working women; statistical trends in divorce, abortion, etc.; changes in family policies; Soviet theoretical and policy discussions; and analyses by Western experts.

In the investigation of the above issues, I have relied on both Soviet and Western sources. Among these sources are official Soviet census and other statistical data; research and discussions of Soviet demographers, economists, and others working in fields related to the population and family problems examined in this paper; and Western research and analyses of Soviet trends. In order to better insure that any gaps or deficiencies in my data would reflect the actual unavailability of data rather than my overlooking such data, I have tried to be as exhaustive as possible in my examination of the scholarly and official materials available in this country.

In addition, I have examined and compared Soviet and Western data for consistency and to find out the kinds of data that are inadequate or not available. For instance, in reading the recent research and discussion by Soviet scholars, they admit that much of their recent research is being undertaken because of the inadequacies in the data that exist. The deficiencies in official information on population and the family are apparently a problem to planners and officials. Western scholars also report areas in which Soviet data are insufficient.

Before proceeding to the first chapter, more attention must be given to the question of the availability and reliability of Soviet data in such sensitive areas as population trends and abortion and divorce, since much of this study depends on Soviet sources. The suspicion that ideological bias may determine the content of Soviet publications or that statistics are misleading, or even false, has been raised frequently enough to prompt comments from several Western demographers. D. Peter Mazur (1973: 46), a well-known expert on Soviet demography, points out that Soviet demographic research does not necessarily follow the Party line. In fact, conclusions "tend to be based strictly on factual information to the extent that its publication is not objectionable to the authorities." I believe that the reader will find, especially in reading chapter 4, that, since 1960, the Soviets have published opinions and data on demographic trends and family policy that could be considered controversial. Established opinions have been challenged and policies criticized. Recognition of "problems" in socialism are also openly discussed. A simple parroting of an official government position does not appear to be the case. No doubt, however, there are limits to Soviet discussions and publication of controversial matters, and the criticisms that do take place do not challenge the basic framework of Marxism-Leninism and socialism.

The quality and accuracy of Soviet demographic data after World War II was assessed by demographer Frank Lorimer (1953: 16-18). Lorimer reported that since 1949, Soviet officials have had "reasonably reliable" data on the population of the USSR "in complete geographical detail, and with a detailed classification by age as well as by sex." This is also true of vital statistics. (It must be added that the Soviets did not begin to publish demographic data after the war until 1950.) This caveat is added, however: "I have never found evidence that any sober official release on population or vital trends in the Soviet Union violates the principle of reportorial fidelity. . . . But this is not enough to guarantee the reliability of the information as a basis of valid inferences. Even reportorially correct releases, if treated un-critically, can lead to fallacious conclusions." It should be remembered that Lorimer was referring to Soviet demographic data published less than 10 years after the end of World War II and at the height of the Cold War. The quality and quantity of Soviet demographic data have improved considerably since that time.

More recently, David Heer (1968: 206), referring to the adequacy of the official vital statistics, remarked that the data are adequate. The biases in registration, for example, have been rather constant over time; therefore, the statistics give a clear picture of gross changes over time. One area where previous registration of births was inadequate was in non-European republics. As late as 1960, births were underrecorded in rural areas to such an extent that urban rates were often higher than rural rates (an unlikely state of affairs). Such underreporting has apparently been largely corrected. (Kvasha, 1974: 20-21)[1].

The main problem I have encountered in my research is that certain kinds of data are not available. Abortion rates and prevalence of contraception usage are two areas where official data are sparse. However, studies have been done in recent years that do allow for some reasonable inferences about the incidence of abortion and contraceptive practices. There is also little data on the prevalence of illegitimacy. On the other hand, I have been quite fortunate in finding information on fertility by age group, region, nationality, and other variables. In the end, of course, perhaps all that can be expected of a researcher is that he present as much data and the best data he can find to answer his questions.

CHAPTER 1

THE ORIGINS AND CONTENT OF SOVIET FAMILY

POLICIES SINCE 1944

The Soviet government's interest in the family is based on both ideological and political grounds. In Soviet history this interest has often been manifested in policies designed to manipulate or coerce the family into behavior favorable to governmental objectives. Soviet family policies since 1944 are no different in this regard since they were a response to postwar economic, demographic, and social problems.

In this chapter, family policies since 1944 dealing with family allowances, abortion and contraception, divorce, illegitimacy, child care, maternity benefits, and motherhood awards will be described along with the general problems the policies were designed to alleviate. This description of the basic content and changes in each policy serves mainly as an introduction. In the following chapters, a detailed analysis of the application and effects of the policies will be given.

As an introduction to the 1944 policies, a brief review of the history of Soviet family policy and population ideology is warranted. (Population ideology receives extensive treatment in chapter 4.)

Family Policies before 1944 and Soviet Population Ideology

The period of the 1920s was characterized by a disregard of the role of the family in society. According to Marx and Engels, the family was to "wither away" once capitalism was replaced by socialism. The family was a vestige of bourgeois social relations, not of the new social order. Besides, in the first decade of the Soviet regime, more immediate concerns than the family faced the government. Most policies that were enacted in the early years, such as freedom of divorce and abortion and rights accorded to unmarried mothers and their offspring,[2] were designed to break down tsarist family practices, especially as they related to the sexes. In contrast to tsarist times, equality of the sexes was a major goal of Soviet policy. Thus legislation was used to secure economic independence for women and to encourage them to enter the labor force. (Schlesinger, 1949: 1)[3]

Other proposals designed to free women for "more productive" social work involved the state's assuming a larger share of the family's traditional childrearing responsibilities. Public dining facilities, child care institutions, and other domestic services were the major proposals suggested. These efforts to weaken the family by eliminating its functions, especially those pertaining to the raising of children, aroused widespread opposition among the Soviet people. The fact that implementing such programs involved enormous expenditures also added to the failure of these proposals to affect more than a tiny portion of the Soviet population.

By the 1930s, negative reactions to the experimentation in sexual freedom and the breakdown of the family were prevalent. Freedom of divorce and abortion seemed to many to be a legitimation of "sex debauchery." (Geiger, 1968: 71) By 1936 family policy began to reflect the conservative mood. For example, divorce and abortion became extremely difficult to obtain and the ideological assessment of the family changed radically. No longer destined to "wither away," the family was to be "strengthened." Geiger (1968: 97) gives several reasons for the shift in policies toward the family. These include (1) the family was needed as an agent of social control; (2) Stalin was eager to gain public support after the hardships of forced collectivization and industrialization; and (3) fear of war led to the desire to increase the birth rate, for which a more stable family life was deemed a prerequisite.

Another reason for Stalin's obsession with high population growth and fertility rates, was ideological. In Marxist population theory, each historical stage is said to have its own characteristic "laws of development." Capitalism is characterized by poverty and unemployment and, therefore, a "relative overpopulation" of workers. This overpopulation was not "absolute" but was the result of inadequate institutions and the capitalist system of distribution. In socialism, however, there would be no poverty or unemployment; thus, population size or growth could not be a problem. Stalin, and Soviet ideology, used high rates of population growth and fertility as evidence of the workers' prosperity and the "socialist law of population." Another reason for Stalin's pro-growth position was the belief in the active role of men in shaping their environment. (This belief also led to the ludicrous Lysenko affair.) Man's ability, and for Stalin this meant the Party's ability, to cope with any problem was considered unlimited. (Petersen, 1975: 672) Population growth was interpreted simply as an increase in the number of workers enlisted in the "struggle against capitalism." Rapid population growth was considered so vital by Stalin that the 1937 census was suppressed because it did not show as much growth as Stalin had expected. As a result, the directors of the census bureau reportedly were executed and the 1939 census was commissioned. (Dallin, 1947: 132)

In summary, Soviet family policy after 1936 was a radical departure from the position held in the 1920s. After 1936, Soviet family policy became increasingly conservative and oriented toward providing a stable family that would be supportive of the regime and its programs. As Inkeles and Bauer (1968: 192) point out, the family was now regarded as essential to society both as an inculcator of socialist values and as the bearer of "many children." As we shall see, Soviet family policy after World War II retained much of this prewar conservative orientation. However, postwar problems and societal developments necessitated many important changes and additions in family policy.

Family Policies Since 1944

It would be difficult to overstate the devasting effects of World War II on the Soviet population and society. Stalin himself acknowledged that from 12-19 million people were killed during the war. Furthermore, the loss of males was so great that 14 years after the war there were still over 20 million more Soviet women than men. (Petersen, 1964: 120-21) This population loss does not include the deficit of births during the war years when fertility levels were extremely low. The total deficit due to mortality and birth deficits during and immediately after World War II is estimated at 45 million. (Petersen, 1975: 703) The inauguration of the 1944 policies on the family can be looked upon as a direct response to the wartime destruction.

The 1944 laws were heralded as a means to strengthen the family and promote large families. As Sverdlov (in Inkeles, 1968: 217-18), a prominent Soviet family law expert, reportedly said, it is in society's interest to

9

have a "strong, many-childrened family." Soviet desires to strengthen the family were not ends in themselves. Policy toward the family, argues Petersen (1969: 670-71) is determined largely by the government's own interests. The goals of Soviet family policies in the postward period were to increase the birth rate and alleviate the burdens of families with children in order to encourage greater labor force participation from the population. Not only were lower fertility rates a threat to future labor force needs, but the deficit of men in the population meant that the current labor force demands had to be filled by women.[5]

To reiterate, the 1944 policies can be viewed as having a dual function: (1) to alleviate the childrearing burdens of the family, especially women, in order to increase female labor force participation; and (2) to encourage women to bear children without withdrawing from the labor force. As mentioned above, the particular policies selected were designed to fulfill one or both of these goals. Each policy will be discussed in turn along with subsequent changes.

a. Family Allowances

The payments made to families with children have often been regarded as one of the most pronatalist policies in the Soviet Union. Beginning in 1944, the state began to pay 200 (old) rubles on the birth of each child. This lump sum increased with each additional child up to 2500 rubles for the 11th and all subsequent births. Moreover, 40 to 150 rubles per month, depending on the number of children, were also paid. This monthly payment only continued, however, until the child's fifth birthday. (Geiger and Inkeles, 1954: 401) Children of unmarried mothers also received payments, as will be discussed in the section below on illegitimacy.

10

Along with income tax exemptions, which had been granted in 1943-44 for families with children,[6] the family allowance program was of considerable benefit to many families. The tax exemption plus the grant for the fourth child, for example, equaled 30% of the average annual wage in 1944. For the eleventh child, the sum was 98% of the average wage. And since payments were often received for more than one child, the total payments could exceed considerably the yearly wage. As an example, if a woman's fifth, sixth, and seventh child was between the ages of one to five, three monthly stipends were given that ranged from 120-200 (new) rubles. (Dodge, 1966:23)

Effective January 1, 1948, family allowances were cut in half. This change invited several explanations from Western scholars, although most agree that the Soviets had not suddenly assumed an antinatalist position. One explanation for the reduction in payments is that the increase in average annual wage plus income tax reductions diminished the need for allowances. (Dodge, 1966: 23) Another exaplantion is that the crop failures of 1946 and food shortages in subsequent years made the encouragement of large families an unfeasible policy. (Cook, 1967: 94) Finally, Heer (1968: 234) argues that the policy had become increasingly ineffective as a spur to higher fertility. It is very likely, however, that the cost of the program was a significant factor in the cutbacks. Between 1945-50 the number of recipients of payments for four or more children more than tripled--from 844,000 to 3,079,000. (Vestnik statistiki, No. 11, 1967: 83)

A final factor in the reduction in payments relates back to the dual function of Soviet family policy, i.e., to encourage both childbearing and female labor force participation. A family allowance that was large relative to wages might actually encourage women to drop out of or not to enter the

11

labor force. If, on the other hand, wages were high relative to family allowances, women might be more likely to join the labor force, even if they were
receiving allowances for children.

At any rate, there can be little doubt that recent schedules of family
allowance payments are not nearly as significant a pronatalist measure as they
were in 1944. Heer and Bryden (1966: 156) calculated that family payments as
a percentage of average annual income steadily declined since 1944. For
instance, in 1944 payment for the birth of the 5th child when the 4th child
was 1-4 years old amounted to 50.5% of the average wage. In 1948 payments
were only 19% of the average wage; the figure for 1964 was 12.3%[7]. Moreover,
the increase in the number of mothers receiving payments slowed down considerably since 1950, when over 3 million mothers of four or more children were
receiving payments. By 1960 the number of mothers increased to 3,455,000; in
1967 mothers receiving payments increased to only 3,529,000. (Vestnik
statistiki, No. 11, 1967: 83)

The number of mothers receiving stipends is considerable, however. As
the table below indicates, mothers in each category have increased since 1945.

Number of Mothers Receiving Monthly Stipends
for Four or More Children
(in thousands)

	1945	1960	1966	1967
Total	844	3455	3541	3529
With 4 children	287	1660	1508	1447
5	181	899	885	877
6	100	484	560	572
7 or more	276	412	588	633

(TsSU, 1967: 265; Vestnik statistiki, No. 11, 1967: 83)

b. Abortion and Contraception

In 1936 legal abortion had been made very difficult to obtain in the USSR, but after 1944 it was virtually impossible except for medical reasons. As with other family policies in 1944, the law was designed to increase the birth rate and population growth as a result of wartime population losses.

The law was changed in 1955, and abortion was relegalized. The Soviets issued various explanations for this sudden reversal in policy. One reason given was that women should be allowed the choice in motherhood. Another explanation focused on protecting the health of the mother by eliminating the harm of illegal abortions. The first explanation is hardly adequate. As Petersen (1975: 710) remarks, Soviet policies have never been geared toward the family's interests or "right to choose." The state's interests have indicated family policy. The state's interest in the case of abortion is obvious from a statement by B. Urlanis (1963: 33): not only was illegal abortion a threat to the mother's health, it was also a threat to the economy which was so dependent on female participation. Absenteeism, ill health, and death of the mother and/or the child were too often the results of illegal abortions. The reason for legalizing abortion was, in short, to control it.

The relegalization of abortion, as well as some other policy changes,[8] led to some speculation that the Soviets were not pronatalist or that they pursued contradictory policies. Heer and Bryden (1966: 514) are proponents of this interpretation of Soviet policy. I would question this interpretation for several reasons. For one, the relegalization of abortion was accompanied by other measures that were pronatalist. For instance, in 1956 benefits to pregnant women were increased, family allowances were still in effect, and child care facilities were expanded.[9] Secondly, Soviet population theory

13

(see chapter 4) and propaganda were adamantly pronatalist during this period. Sauvy (1963: 255) quotes Khrushchev in 1955 speaking to a group of Soviet young people:

> A man who founds a family is a good citizen. Our country will become all the stronger with a more numerous population. . . .

And in justifying the tax on bachelors and childless families, Khruschev said the following:

> . . . If each family has only one or two children, the population will not increase, it will decline. But the development of society is our concern. That is why a family must have three children and all will be well! . . .

Moreover, during this period, the Soviets were carrying on a particularly virulent attack against the principle of family planning and birth control. (Cf. Petersen, 1964) As Robert Cook (1952: 26) suggests, the attack on family planning had as its purpose ". . . to persuade the Russian people that the choice of a small family--and of a controlled population--is synonymous with warfare, murder, and depravity. By using interchangeably the ideas of genocide and of controlled fertility, the wickedness of a lowered birth rate is powerfully expressed in the Soviet line of talk."

The Soviet hostility toward birth control, despite the relegalization of abortion, is also suggested by the suppression of contraceptives in the USSR during this time. According to Sauvy (in Cook, 1952: 21), the sale and manufacture of contraceptives was probably no longer sanctioned after the 1944 laws were instituted. Although no data for this period is available, recent Soviet complaints about the population's ignorance in the use and availability of contraceptives suggests that only in more recent years have such devices been widely available. (Cf. Sadvokasova, 1968: 223) Mehlan (1966: 213) remarks that contraceptives are not widely used. Almost 40% of women who have had an abortion use no contraception. If they have tried contraceptives and failed (i.e., become pregnant), they do not try contraceptives again. Soviet sources all acknowledge that even in recent years, and despite government support of contraception as an alternative to abortion, abortion is still far more preferred by Societ women. Reasons for recent government support of contraception will be discussed in chapter 3.

c. Divorce

Stricter divorce laws originally had been enacted in the 1930s, but in 1944 even more obstacles were placed before couples seeking to end their marriages. The reason for this law was to promote stability in the family and, hopefully, increase the birth rate. One change in the law was a sizable fee charged for a divorce. The application alone cost 10 rubles. The divorce, when granted, cost one or both parties 50-200 rubles. (Riasentsev, 1967: 120-21) Also people seeking divorce had to go before a people's tribunal, where attempts were made to reconcile the couples. If reconciliation failed, couples were sent to superior court, where their cases were heard and divorce granted or denied. Another measure to discourage divorce was the entering of a divorce on the person's passport.[10] (Petersen, 1964: 11-12)

Soviet authorities generally denied that the new policy toward divorce was actually designed to end divorce or make it virtually impossible to obtain. Sverdlov (in Schlesinger, 1949: 379), for instance, claimed that the new law was designed to prevent "lightmindedness" toward marriage--although he added that this did not imply preventing divorce when both parties agree. Sverdlov contended that only 5-6% of divorces were rejected and that these were all suits where one party contested (of which about 23% were rejected).

15

Western opinion differs from Sverdlov on the availability of divorce after the new law was passed. Geiger and Inkeles (1954: 402) counter that divorce was usually granted only if the marriage was already actually dissolved or chances of reconciliation remote (due to insanity, desertion, or similar circumstances). Petersen (1964: 111) goes so far as to claim that after 1944, all but political reasons were eliminated as absolute grounds for divorce. It is also admitted, however, that most of the population seemed to favor the new law because irresponsibility in family life had resulted from more liberal policies in the past. (Geiger and Inkeles, 1954: 402)

There were grounds for opposition to the new law, however, and these increased over time. For one, the new law made it prohibitively expensive for low income couples to get a divorce. Designed to stabilize the family, it was feared that the new law would, instead, lead to delay of marriage, free love, and adultery. (Coser, 1951: 430) This fear was apparently borne out in many cases. According to Kurganov (1967: 123-24), the Soviet press was full of accounts of the "extraordinary, even monstrous complexity" of the new divorce process. Marriages were dissolved and new families begun while divorce cases were bogged down in court and left unsettled, sometimes for years. Thus the new unions and the resultant children were legally illegitimate.

The law was finally liberalized in 1965, mainly because it had failed to curb divorces. Also the courts were seldom successful in reconciling couples. (Kurganov, 1967: 125) On the contrary, the earlier law apparently created more problems than it solved through the proliferation of illegitimate unions. The main changes in the 1965 law were that only one court, the people's court, was involved in the divorce, and the obligatory publishing of the divorce was abolished. Also the required number of documents and certificates was decreased.

(Kurganov, 1967: 124-25)

Further liberalization of the divorce law occurred in 1968. Couples
with no children were now allowed to obtain a divorce by sending a postcard to
the local registration office. After a 60-day waiting period, the divorce was
granted. (Novoe v zakonodatel'stvo, 1970: 32)

The liberalization of the divorce law should not be taken as a sign of
the government's decision that divorce is no longer its concern. There is
alarm about the high rate of divorce lowering the birth rate. (Cook, 1967: 95)
A recent statement by Gorkin (1969: 48) illustrates the Soviet concern about
the impact of divorce on childbearing:

> Socialist society is giving much attention to the protection
> and encouragement of motherhood and to guaranteeing a happy child-
> hood. This is why judges and people's assessors have to display
> special care, sensitivity, and responsibility in dealing with
> questions of family and marital relationships. It must not be
> forgotten that the reason why a marriage breaks up is not a matter
> of indifference to the state and to our society. An unjustified
> divorce may affect not only personal but social interests.

d. Illegitimacy

Legislation affecting illegitimate children and unwed mothers also
underwent a change in 1944. One of the major changes was that unmarried
mothers could no longer claim support from the alleged father, nor could the
father's surname be given to the child. Moreover, an illegitimate child could
no longer inherit on an equal basis with registered (legal) children. On the
other hand, the state began to provide substantial payments to unmarried
mothers. According to Schlesinger (1949: 401), the amount paid by the state
was comparable to the payments previous legislation required of a father with
an income of 400-500 (old) rubles per month, i.e., the pay of a semi-skilled

town worker or an average-skilled village worker. In addition, state payments were given until the child was 12 years old, plus the same family allowances paid to other mothers of over three children were paid for illegitimate children. (Coser, 1951: 427)[11] Other state aid provided for illegitimate children included the option to place the child in a children's institution for upbringing at the state's expense. (Sverdlov, 1950: 197)

The purported reason for the new policy was that the family should be established as the nurturer of individual and social growth in Soviet society. (Madison, 1963: 90) Some observers suggest other reasons for the Soviet policy shift. The policy had clear connections with the Soviet desire to increase the birth rate. The lopsided sex ratio after World War II, showing a large deficit of young men, meant that many women capable of bearing children could not find a marriage partner. Thus, unmarried motherhood was encouraged by the payments provided for out-of-wedlock children. (Schlesinger, 1949: 406) Also the abolition of child support for illegitimate children was designed to encourage male extramarital involvement. If the father has to pay for his children, he is more likely to avoid unmarried women. (Mace, 1963: 243)

Support payments for illegitimate children were finally abolished in the 1960s. According to the government, 8 million were on the rolls and the costs were too great to maintain the program. (Cook, 1967: 95) It would be interesting to find out the number of illegitimate children produced from the illegal unions of couples that resulted from repressive divorce legislation. Also notable, at the time the payments were abolished, the sex ratio for the population of childbearing age was becoming more proportionate. It is reasonable that supporting illegitimacy in order to encourage higher birth rates was no longer considered necessary.

e. Child Care Facilities and Maternity Benefits

Providing child care facilities and maternity benefits to families has long been a feature of Soviet family policy. After the abolition of abortion in 1936, such aid was increased in order to encourage fertility levels. (Guins, 1954: 300) After World War II, the government expanded child care facilities, especially in urban areas (see chapter 2), hoping that this policy would enable parents with children to work and would encourage working couples to have children. In 1948 the costs of maintenance in kindergartens and nurseries were reduced 25% for families with 2 children and earnings up to 60 rubles per month; 50% for those with 3 children and up to 80 rubles income; and 50% reductions were given to families with 4 or more children regardless of income. Single mothers earning up to 60 rubles paid only 40% of the maintenance cost of their children. (Dodge, 1966: 81) By 1967 there were 8,534,000 children in nurseries and kindergartens in the USSR. (Novoe v zakonodatel'stvo, 1970: 18)

Provision of these facilities has not, however, kept pace with demand (see chapter 2). Since the 1960s, enrollments in boarding schools and schools of the prolonged day (8:00 a.m. to 7:00 p.m.) have also grown rapidly. Most of these facilities are located in urban areas and their popularity is expected to increase. (Bronfenbrenner, 1968: 116)

In 1944 maternity benefits for working women were increased. For 6 weeks after the birth of a child a woman was to receive pay equal to from 50-100% of her wages. The size of payments usually depended on the length of time on the job, union membership, or the status of the job. Previously, such payments were given for only 4 weeks. Women were also allowed 5 weeks leave before the birth of a child and 2 extra weeks for abnormal or multiple births.

Layette benefits increased from 45 to 120 rubles; nursing benefits from 90 to 180 rubles. The law covered all working women except collective farm workers, domestic workers, and a few other minor categories of workers. (Dodge, 1966: 67-69)

In 1956 maternity leave was increased from 77 to 112 days (56 days before birth and 56 days after). Other changes allowed a new mother to take an additional 3 months unpaid leave and then return to her job without loss of pay or status. If a woman quit her job but returned within a year, she could retain her status of "working consecutively" (important in receiving many benefits). Also, the minimum benefit pay was set at 2/3 of the woman's average earnings even for nonunion women. (Dodge, 1966: 72-73) The 1970-75 Five-Year Plan calls for even greater expansion of these benefits. (Vzhilianskii, 1973: 53)

These child care and maternity benefits indicate the state's interest in making work and childbearing compatible roles for Soviet women.

f. Motherhood Awards

A series of awards for mothers of five or more children was inaugurated by the Soviets in 1944. Three categories of awards are given. The first is the Medal of Motherhood given to women with 5-6 children. The second is that of Glorious Motherhood given to mothers of 7-9 children. The last, and highest, award is that of Mother Heroine. This award goes to mothers of 10 or more children. Although largely honorific, the recognition of motherhood by the state and treating the bearing of many children as a public service lent much normative status to large families. Unfortunately, there are little data on the distribution or method of determining award recipients. (See Heer and Bryden, 1966)

20

Below is a table listing the number of recipients of these awards from 1944-70. Although the number of recipients in each category has increased, it is not clear why this has been the case; i.e., whether the increases represent better registration of mothers in high fertility regions, larger families, or simply normal increments due to population growth. It could not be inferred from this data alone, that the increase in recipients indicates the success of family policy in encouraging fertility. The data are presented simply as a matter of information on the number of motherhood award recipients since the program began.

Motherhood Award Recipients: 1944-70
(in thousands)

	1944-49	1950-60	1961-70
Mother Heroine	31	34	73
Glorious Motherhood			
1st degree	67	89	184
2nd degree	193	228	413
3rd degree	468	534	817
Medal of Motherhood			
1st degree	754	1073	1398
2nd degree	1434	2032	2180

(TsSU, 1967: 265; Vestnik statistiki, No. 11, 1967: 84 and No. 1, 1972: 92)

The above description of the various family policies indicates the government's concern with an increase in fertility in the USSR and with higher participation of women in the labor force. The discussion so far gives little reason as to why these particular policies were chosen or at whom they were directed. If we can assume that a family policy, in order to be successful, must take into account the interests and circumstances of families (insofar as these interests and circumstances are understood), then understanding Soviet family policy requires that we examine the Soviet postwar society in which

21

families are situated. Furthermore, it is important to note any fundamental differences in family interests or circumstances among the Soviet population. Undoubtedly, family policies directed to one group might be ineffective or irrelevant to another group with dissimilar interests or circumstances. Chapter two is devoted to the problem of the application of family policies to the Soviet population.

CHAPTER 2

THE APPLICATION OF SOVIET FAMILY POLICIES

The point has been made that Soviet family policies were designed to promote both fertility and female employment among Soviet families. But it must be remembered that Soviet families do not comprise a homogeneous group. On the contrary, the Soviet population is heterogeneous in cultural and nationality characteristics as well as in the problems they have faced in Soviet society since World War II. Moreover, fertility and female levels vary significantly among different groups within the population. A family policy that ignored such essential differences in its population could not hope to be successful.

In the USSR the broadest group differences, essential to family policy, are based on rural or urban residence and, in some instances, European or non-European nationality. These groups face different problems and have major cultural differences. These cultural differences can be summed up as differences in level or modernization, e.g., group traditions; material and cultural living standards (both consumption patterns and aspirations); and family structure, especially the position of women.

The following discussion deals with the different problems and circumstances of the urban and rural populations and, where important differences exist, the European and non-European populations; and how these group differences relate to family policy. These population distinctions actually overlap, thus complicating the analysis. For example, discussion of the urban population applies mainly to the Europeans since they comprise most of the urban population. On the other hand, the rural population could be either European or non-European. Although general remarks about the rural population apply to both nationality groups, distinctions between Europeans or non-Europeans are, in some cases, quite important. Not only can the implementation of family policy be linked to these group distinctions, but also the effectiveness of family policy (discussed in chapter 3).

To be more specific, some policies, such as child care, were implemented mainly in urban areas where the need was greatest. Policies such as divorce or abortion laws, while perhaps not directly aimed at urban areas, were mainly applicable to the urban population. The rural population had relatively little divorce or abortion. This is especially true of non-Europeans. By contrast, few urban families were large enough to qualify for family allowances or motherhood awards.

It is not being suggested that the 1944 policies were in all cases purposely designed with a particular population group in mind. Such a position would not be supportable by evidence and also implies a prescience on the part of Soviet policymakers that is doubtful. However, the evidence does indicate that in some cases discriminations in providing benefits or services were deliberate. This does not imply malign intent or stupidity on the part of policymakers. On the contrary, I would suggest that Soviet policymakers acted on the basis of their understanding at the time of the kinds of policies that would achieve their objectives. This required that they consider the basic differences in their population.

As a final introductory note to the following chapter, I wish to point out that I have in most instances emphasized data for years up to 1960 only. The reason is that this is the period in which, for the most part, family policy was formulated. Moreover, it is the period up to 1960 in which we can get an idea of the characteristics of the population to which the various policies applied.

The Urban Population after World War II

Economic development after World War II resulted in a tremendous expansion of urban areas in the USSR. The rapid growth in cities contributed to already inadequate living conditions, and material hardships faced by many families necessitated that women increasingly seek employment outside the home. Tremendous pressures were placed on family life as a consequence of the problems of urban life, and instability in family relations became more prevalent.

a. Rapid growth and industrialization

A significant feature of the postwar situation in the Soviet Union was the tremendous upsurge in industrialization and urbanization. Because the war had taken a devastating toll on the Soviet economy (as well as on the population), a drive to rebuild rapidly was begun. This required, as mentioned previously, that women as well as men be recruited into the urban labor force in unprecedented numbers. In 1946 the deficit of working-age (16-59) men amounted to 20.7 million; the figure was still 15.4 million in 1959. (Dodge, 1966: 30) These figures show how crucial the need was for working women.

The rapid growth of the cities is indicated by the following figures. In 1940 about 33% of the population was classified as urban. In 1950 this figure rose to 40%, and by 1959 the urban population was 48% of the total.

During the period 1939-56 the rural population declined by 18-19 million--about 14%. (Roof and Leedy, 1959: 215) By 1970 the population was 56% urban, and from 1959 to 1970 the urban population grew by 35% over 36 million. (TsSU, Vol. 1, 1972: 5) Most of the new industrial expansion took place in large cities of 100,000 or more. Whereas in 1939 there had been 82 large cities, by 1959 there were 148 large cities. (Khorev, 1968: 97) In 1970 the figure climbed to 220 large cities. (TsSU, Vol. 1, 1972: 22-60)

Another indication of the rapid transition in industrialization and urbanization is the change in occupational class composition. In 1939 industrial workers and service workers comprised 50.2% of the population compared to collective farm workers who were 47.2% of the population. In 1959 the figures were 68.3% and 31.4% respectively (TsSU, 1968: 19); and in 1970--79.3% and 20.5%. (TsSU, Vol. 5, 1973: 9)

b. Living conditions

Conditions in Soviet cities had been appalling before the war, but the new influx of migrants further exacerbated the problems. Sanitary and hygienic conditions worsened, prices rose, and transportation and housing problems grew. (See Khorev, 1968: 100) Living conditions for most urban dwellers were quite spartan. In fact, in terms of municipal utilities, conditions had improved little since 1939, as the table below indicates.

Even in 1960, of 4,713 cities and urban-type settlements, only 75% had a central water system; and of these only 53% had a sewer system too. As for gas, the seven-year plan called for gas for all residential housing only in Moscow, Kiev, and Leningrad by the end of 1965. In the early 1960s, even in Moscow, only 39% of apartments had a bathroom and only 10% had hot running water. (Sosnovy 1962: 176-77)

26

Percent of the Urban Population with Municipal
Utilities: 1939 and 1956

Utility	1939	1956
Electric lighting	84.8	89.3
Running water	38.7	34.0
Central heating	11.1	22.4
Gas		15.6
Bath	7.5	8.9
Hot water	.7	2.2
Plumbing	28.1	31.4

(Geiger, 1968: 207)

Inadequate housing is another major problem facing urban dwellers. Whole
towns had been leveled during the war, and in 1945 close to 18 million people
were living in what Sorlin (1968: 202-03) calls "primitive conditions." The
unprecedented immigration to cities only worsened the crisis. While the privi-
leged population--soldiers, high officials, and essential workers--received a
room for their families, others lived in crowded communal dormitories. Shanty
towns grew up around the large cities.

Conditions were so bad that high labor turnover in crucial economic
sectors was beginning to threaten the fulfillment of economic plans. In 1956,
in response to this crisis, the government launched an ambitious program of
new housing construction. Despite this effort, per capita living space between 1950 and 1960 only increased from 4.67 to 5.26 sq. meters.[12] In urban
centers, the number of persons per room changed from 3.43 in 1950 to 3.04 in
1960. (Sosnovy, 1962: 175-76) Crowding is so severe, according to Hanson
(1968: 66), that the question, "Is the bathroom free?" is usually construed as,
"Is there anybody living in the bathroom?"[13]

Not only were urban living conditions poor after the war, but consumption levels were also greatly reduced. According to Sorlin (1968: 200-01), it

was 1952 before the output of shoes, many clothes, and household implements reached 1940 levels. Food was also a problem since the Germans had destroyed harvests, animals, and villages during their retreat. Only in 1953 did cattle and pig production reach 1940 levels. In 1946-47 thousands of people starved and the prices for many food items tripled.

Wages during the late 1940s were not able to keep up with the cost of living. By 1948 real weekly wages dropped about 40% from 1938 in terms of purchasing power although the number of working hours increased considerably. The average family survived by having several salaried workers in the family. (Schwarz, 1948: 282-86) This meant, apparently, that the Soviet goal of getting women into the labor force was being achieved through necessity as much or more than by positive inducements.

c. Women in the labor force

Female labor force participation was encouraged from the beginning of the Soviet period. Ideologically, the woman's right to work was considered a prerequisite for her emancipation--especially from dependence on males. Soviet policy was, in many respects, designed to give women equal rights and privileges with males. However, as Geiger (1968: 59-60) suggests, this policy of encouraging women to work often led to a worsening rather than improvement in their status. For one, most women were illiterate and accustomed to being submissive. Few women utilized their new rights nor did they pursue equality. In urban families, the woman usually worked only out of necessity. Moreover, even among women who worked, most of the housework and child care functions were performed by the woman. Services and appliances to lighten this burden on the women were usually unavailable. This created a tremendous hardship for the working wife--a problem still not resolved in the USSR (see chapter 3).

28

Although family policy was designed to promote both motherhood and the worker role for women, these goals are often hard to reconcile. Women with children are usually less likely to work than are single or childless women due to their responsibilities in the home. Also women who work are more likely to keep their family size small since they have less time to care for the family's needs.[14]

Family Policies

The problems in urban areas of family instability and combining the work and domestic roles of women were met by several policies: divorce laws, abortion and contraceptive policies, and child care and maternity benefits. It was hoped that restricting divorce would keep families together and that aid to mothers would lighten their domestic burdens. Incentives to childbearing as well as prohibiting the means to preventing births would encourage mothers to have more children.

a. Divorce laws

The problems of urban living have contributed to the frequency of divorce in the USSR.[15] When laws were passed to make divorce more difficult and to "stabilize" and "strengthen" the family, it was the urban family, especially in the European republics, that was being addressed. The 1949 divorce rates show that divorce had been overwhelmingly an urban phenomenon. Whereas there was one divorce per 575 rural marriages, there was one divorce per 90 urban marriages. The disparities were even greater in the 1950s. In 1953 there was a divorce for every 50 urban compared to 736 rural marriages; in 1957 one divorce occurred for every 32 urban and every 640 rural marriages. (Kurganov, 1967: 192)

Statistics on divorce by republic in 1967 (I have not found any earlier statistics) further indicate that divorce has been largely an urban, European phenomenon. The national rate of divorce per 1000 population was 2.7. All of the republics above or near this average were European republics, but every non-European republic was well below the national average. All of the capital cities within the republics showed divorce rates close to or far in excess of the national average. In the European republics, those that are over 50% urban in the 1970 census were above the national average in divorce in 1967; those that are predominantly rural had divorce rates below the national average. (There is no such correlation for non-European republics.)

1967 Divorce Rates in the Republics of the USSR and Capital Cities (per thousand population)

Republic	1967	Republic	1967
RSFSR	3.2	Azerbaidzhan	1.4
Moscow	5.9	Baku	3.5
Ukraine	3.0	Armenia	1.0
Kiev	5.4	Erevan	2.2
Lithuania	1.8	Uzbek	1.1
Vil'niuse	3.2	Tashkent	3.8
Latvia	4.2	Kirgiz	1.1
Riga	6.3	Frunze	3.3
Moldavia	2.2	Tadzhik	1.1
Kishinev	5.6	Dushanbe	3.3
Estonia	3.2	Turkmen	1.3
Tallin	4.6	Ashkhabad	3.6
Georgia	1.0	Kazakh	1.6
Tbilisi	2.3	Alma-Ata	4.3
Belorussia	1.8		
Minsk	3.4		

(Solov'ev, 1970: 117)

b. Abortion and contraception

Conscious control of family size by the family (family planning) has been typically an urban phenomenon. In the 1930s, according to Kulischer (1948: 96-97) and Maurer (1944: 244-45), abortion largely affected urban

30

women in the larger cities. Government efforts to promote contraception instead of abortion were not very successful. Most women considered abortion
easier. After the prohibition of abortion in 1936, however, women were forced
to learn more about family planning and contraception. (Maurer, 1944: 244-45)
The urban woman's dependence on abortion to limit births is reflected in the
increase in births that occurred in the large cities a year after the 1936 law
was passed.

Increase in Births in Selected Large Cities
in 1937   (1936 = 100)

City	Increase in Births	City	Increase in Births
Moscow	193	Ashkhabad	171
Leningrad	185	Dushanabe	172
Kiev	143	Baku	155
Minsk	141	Tbilisi	152
Khar'kov	175	Frunze	142
Rostov-na-Donu	174		

(Pisarev, 1962: 183)

Although the above table does not give the actual number of births, it does
indicate that births increased sharply--from 41-93%--in the cities mentioned.
The number of births in 1936 is given as 100; the table indicates the number
one year later.

The prohibition of abortion was accompanied by an expansion of child
care facilities and benefits to women who bore children. (Maurer, 1944: 245)
For a time, the urban birth rate increased, but this success was short lived.
Soviet experts Urlanis (1963: 29) and Sadvokasova (1968: 209-10) both point
out that fertility declined steadily within two years after abortion was prohibited. This was due to an increase in both registered and illegal abortion
as well as contraceptive practices.

However, the initial successes of the 1936 abortion policy and child care programs may have contributed to the formulation of the 1944 policies. In 1944 greater restrictions were put on abortions, and child care and maternity benefits were greatly expanded. Contraceptive sale and manufacture were apparently banned. (Cook, 1952: 21) All of these measures could be construed as an effort to leave no alternative to childbearing. These measures would also provide aid, however, to working women once they had a child.

In 1955 the abortion law was repealed and abortion once again became legal. This did not signal a reversal in Soviet family policy goals. Instead, it became apparent that the 1944 prohibition of abortion was not workable. Urban fertility levels declined from a crude birth rate of 26.0 in 1950 to 23.5 in 1955[16] while rural rates were stable--27.1 and 27.4 (Volkov, 1972: 111) Soviet women were resorting to illegal abortion on a large scale. Relegalizing abortion was considered a lesser evil. As one Soviet source remarked, no government can change the fact that women are planning their families and that many of them rely on abortion. Forbidding abortion is not the answer to the abortion issue. (Sadvokasova, 1968: 223) Forbidding abortion also proved not to be the answer to increasing fertility levels.

c. Child care and maternity benefits

Soviet family policies were in part designed to reconcile the Soviet woman's seemingly contradictory roles of worker and mother. In urban areas the working mother was greatly in need of the child care facilities and maternity benefits promised in 1944. And indeed, these benefits were more generously supplied to urban women. As mentioned in chapter 1, maternity benefits were not extended to collective farm women in the 1944 law that provided pay and other benefits for parturient women and new mothers. Also extra benefits were given to mothers with stable, long term job records, thus encouraging their continuation in the labor force after the birth of children. By contrast, Dodge (1966: 69, 73) calls collective farm worker benefits "distinctly inferior." After the 1956 reform, collective farm women were even excluded from receiving the small layette allowance paid urban working women.

Child care facilities have also been disproportionately provided to urban areas. By 1961 only 10% of the nurseries and kindergartens were located on collective farms; most were in urban centers. (Dodge, 1966: 98) In 1965 over 80% of children in preschool facilities lived in cities and towns. (Osborn, 1970: 57-58) The following table shows that between 1940 and 1956 the number of places available to rural children in 1956 was the same as it had been in 1940. It should be kept in mind that during this period well over half the Soviet population was rural not urban in residence.

Number of Places in Permanent Nurseries
in Urban and Rural Areas
(in thousands)

Year	Urban	Rural
1940	523.8	300.3
1950	470.1	265.0
1955	567.6	283.4
1956	604.0	300.3

(data after 1956 is not available)

(Dodge, 1966: 78)

The quality of nurseries also varies between urban and rural areas. Dodge (1966: 82) claims, "As a general rule, rural nurseries are smaller, less well equipped, and less adequately staffed. As a result, the care and training of the children suffer by comparison with urban facilities. In the more remote and backward parts of the Soviet Union the facilities are even more primitive, although they may be as good as, or better than, the homes from which the children come."

This brings us to the rural population of the USSR and the characteristics that distinguish it from the urban population. It will be seen that family policies apply differently to these two population group.

The Rural Population after World War II

The rural population has been both materially and culturally different from the urban population. Rural life has been virtually synonymous with backwardness, even primitiveness. (Feldmesser, 1968: 186) The standard of living in most rural areas is much below that of urban areas, and culturally the Soviet peasant has been less affected by the forces of modernization that have occurred in the USSR. These material and cultural differences, to be discussed below, have had much to do with fertility trends and the labor force participation of women as well as with the family policies most applicable to the rural population.

a. Rural poverty

Material poverty has long been the lot of the Russian peasant. More importantly, a tremendous gap has existed between living conditions in rural as compared to urban areas. In its efforts to industrialize, the Soviet government has exacted enormous sacrifices from the agricultural sector. Most of the advantages of modernization accrued to the urban population--a pattern continued after World War II. In fact, Millar (1971: xiii) claims, "Relatively, if not absolutely, the Soviet rural community was more backward both technically and socially in 1953 than had been the case at the close of the NEP."[17]

Income is one important area of inequality between peasants and urban

34

workers. In 1953 workers on state farms had an average yearly income that was a little more than half that of the average urban worker's wage. On collective farms, the average wage was about 18% of the average urban wage.[18] (Bronson and Krueger, 1971: 229)

The disparity between worker and collective farm incomes is not one simply of direct income. A farm worker has to build his own house and bathroom from his own income, receives no pension from the state,[19] has no public laundry service, and has few kindergartens or nurseries. (Aitov, 1969: 136) Even in the 1960s farm workers received only 1/3 of the annual production of consumer goods. One third of collective farms had no electricity. (Vucinich, 1971: 313) By contrast, in 1958 state expenditures on pensions, health care, education and cultural facilities, public services, etc. for workers and service workers equaled one third of their average direct wages. The proportion spent for farm workers is much smaller. (Aitov, 1969: 316)

b. Cultural backwardness

The rural population is also far behind the urban population culturally. For one, most rural families have maintained a rather traditional social and family structure. According to Selivanov (1969: 143-47), many collective farm families are organized as in tsarist times. There is still a family head that in many ways controls the family groups within the collective. The extended family structure is still strong.

The role of women in the family has also remained highly traditional. Subservience to the husband and mother-in-law persists despite social norms of female emancipation and equality of the sexes. It is not, however, uncommon to find that a woman heads the household. (Selivanov, 1969: 141-47) This is no doubt related to the loss of males in World War II.

The rural woman's low social position is perpetuated, in part, by her low educational and occupation level. In 1959 four-fifths of collective farm women (and 3/4 of men) had no more than an incomplete 7th grade education. Half of the women working on collective farms had less than a 4-year education. Dodge (1971: 193) concludes, "Collective farm women, despite rapid advances in their education, remain educationally the most backward of the major socioeconomic groups." Occupationally, rural women fare no better. In 1959 about 97% were engaged in physical labor. Of these, 83% were employed in unskilled work, mostly highly seasonal field work. The rest of the time they cared for the private plots, the children, and household chores. This pattern of labor force participation pertains to state farm workers as well. The result has been that women have often been kept from acquiring the skills and education that would allow them to get better jobs. (Dodge, 1971: 182-84)[20]

The cultural backwardness of the rural areas has also been related to the general lack of educational resources and achievement. Schools are generally poor in rural areas and the environment in the home is often unfavorable for pursuing education. This results mainly from the fact that many children are assigned farm duties at an early age. Thus, they have inadequate time for school work. (Vucinich, 1971: 314)

The result of inadequate educational resources has been a wide gap between the rural and urban population in educational achievement. In 1962 an estimated 40% of industrial workers, but only 23% of collective farmers, had secondary or higher education. (Miller, 1965: 99) In a 1963 study of children in Novosibirsk, only 10% of collective and state farm children who graduated secondary school wished or were able to go on to full time schooling. By

36

contrast, 82% of the children of urban specialists and 61% of the children of industrial workers were being accepted at specialized or higher educational schools. (Specific reasons for the differences were not given.) Other studies show similar findings. (See Dodge, 1971: 197-201; Vucinich, 1971: 313)

c. High fertility values

The traditionalism of the rural family structure is reflected in rural fertility. The relationship between high fertility and traditional, rural cultural values is widely known, and the USSR is no exception. Large families have been customary. Data on completed fertility for 1960 show that over 62% of rural women had 3 or more children compared to about 46% of urban women. Less than 1/4 of urban women had more than 3 children; almost 1/2 of rural women did. (Vestnik statistiki, No. 8, 1967: 93) Age at marriage, a variable often associated with fertility, has also been substantially lower in rural areas. In 1962 about 53% of rural women were married between the ages of 20-24 compared to 35% of workers and 24% of service workers. (Urlanis, 1963: 66)

In rural families, family planning was, on the whole, an unheard of practice. According to Geiger (1968: 196), peasants looked upon children as "natural" and the "will of God." They did not use or know about contraception, and abortion was seen by most as an abomination. When birth control was practiced, it was mainly abortion under primitive conditions. The reasons for the lack of family planning were that children were often seen as a source of old age security; and, since few expectations about social mobility were held, there was really little source of motivation for family limitation. (see chapter 3 for a discussion of social mobility and family limitation.)

Family Policies

The social structure of the rural areas should make Soviet family policies more understandable. The above discussion shows that policies directed toward a "stable family" would not be necessary for the rural population. And abortion and contraceptive usage were already low and would require little regulation as in urban areas. In addition, since rural women have traditionally played the roles of worker and mother with little conflict, extensive child care facilities and maternity benefits would not be as necessary. Family allowances and motherhood awards, on the other hand, were applicable to the rural areas.

Family Allowances and Motherhood Awards

Since wages and living conditions in rural areas were so depressed compared to urban standards, family allowances--even after the 1947 reductions--could have been a substantial incentive to have more children. We should keep in mind that during the 1940s and 1950s there were few of the pressures to lower fertility that existed in urban areas. It was mentioned above that most rural women had more than three children. Family allowances were perhaps considered an added incentive to ensure that rural women would continue to have large numbers of children.

Motherhood awards, although alone an insufficient incentive to have larger families, provided publicity and enhanced the status of women with many children. This moral-propagandistic measure would be a useful addition to the economic incentives provided by family allowances.[21] (Such an approach is advocated by some recent population planners, as will be discussed in chapter 4.)

Family allowances and motherhood awards are less applicable to the urban than to the rural population because urban fertility and family sizes have not been as great. Rural families have had a far larger proportion of the large families that qualify for family allowances and motherhood awards. In 1959 (the first figures available) over 31% of rural families had over 4 members compared to 21% of urban families. (Urlanis, 1963: 71) More revealing than family size (which includes other persons than nuclear family members), 1960 statistics on completed family size showed that about 46% of urban women had 3 or more children (about 23% of these had only 3 children), but more than 62% of rural women had 3 or more children by the end of their childbearing years (almost 49% of these had more than 3 children). Three children is the minimum to qualify for any family allowance (a small lump sum at the birth of the third child). Four children are necessary in order to receive monthly payments. Large families of over 4 children are overwhelmingly rural. Only 14% of urban families had 5 children or more; 37% of rural families had 5 or more children. (Vestnik statistiki, No. 8, 1967: 93) Five children is the minimum number for which motherhood awards are given.

The non-European Population

The general discussion above of the Soviet rural and urban populations needs some qualification. There are some important differences in the urban and rural populations based on European or non-European nationality. The European republics have been the leaders in economic and social development in the USSR and have been most exposed to modernizing influences. Non-European republics have been last in this process. In addition, considerable immigration of European nationalities, especially Russians, to these republics has been occurring. Soviet family policies apply differently in some cases

depending on whether or not the population is of European or non-European
nationality.

a. Traditional culture

The European and non-European populations of the USSR are distinct
groups in significant respects. The Europeans--mainly Russian, Ukrainian,
Belorussian, Estonian, Lithuanian, Latvian, Moldavian, and Georgian--are mostly
located in the western half of the country in the republics that bear their
names. The European population is culturally more similar to the West than to
the Asian East. The non-European population--inhabitants of the Armenian,
Azerbaidzhan, Kazakh, Uzbek, Turkmen, Tadzhik, and Kirgiz SSR's (republics)
as well as several autonomous republics--are more Asian in culture. The non-
Europeans have preserved their traditional agrarian way of life and have been
relatively untouched by the industrial growth and social change occurring in
the western parts of the country. The extended family predominates along with
an emphasis on high fertility to preserve the family line. Life style is
governed by religious (mainly Moslem or Buddhist) precepts. Essentially, the
non-Europeans are characterized by social and economic underdevelopment.
(Mazur, 1967A: 182-84)

b. European migration to cities

Although the non-Europeans have been the least modern group in the
Soviet population, a great deal of economic development is taking place in the
non-European republics, especially in urban areas. The large cities face many
of the same problems discussed above in the section on the urban population.
In some cases, problems are even more acute in the non-European than in the
European cities. The standard of living in terms of living space, goods and

services, and food supplies in some regions has been considerably worse than in the Moscow region, for example, despite the fact that wages are higher. (Bernard, 1966: 200)

Among the most important features of urbanization of the non-European republics is that much of the growth has been due to European immigration, not to the influx of the rural, native population. In 1959 of all the non-European republics, only in Azerbaidzhan and Armenia did the native population make up the majority of the urban population. Russians alone were about 1/3 to 1/2 of the urban population in most republics. (Bondarskaia, 1970: 174) The European composition of the cities of the non-European republics has important bearing on some family policy measures, as discussed below.

Family Policies

There is no evidence as to whether or not the Soviets took into account the differences between the European or non-European populations in conceiving or implenting family policy. If anything, family policy may have been developed mainly with the European population in mind. Europeans played the major role in Soviet development; the non-European republics underwent most of their development only after World War II. Europeans are the vast majority of the population--over 80%. Moreover, it is Europeans who play the predominant role in the urban, industrial economy, the sector of the economy that has had the greatest priority. And it is in industry, not agriculture, that female employment has been so sorely needed. Finally, it was the European population that suffered the greatest population loss and low fertility during World War II. All of these facts suggest that encouraging the birth rate and female employment were initially aimed mainly at the European population.

However, as was mentioned, many Europeans were migrating to cities in non-European republics. The high priority given to developing the East was reflected in the provision of child care facilities. In rural areas, non-Europeans began receiving many motherhood awards, and their large families made them eligible for family allowances.

a. Child care

As is true for the rural and urban areas in general, the provision of child care facilities varies by rural-urban areas in the Asian republics. For instance, in 1959 in Tuckmen SSR, only 13.3% of children of kindergarten age could be accommodated in kindergartens; but in the highly urban Charzhouskii region, 45.1% of kindergarten age children could be accommodated. At the same time, only 8% and 10.9% could be accommodated in the rural Maryiskii and Tashauzkii regions, respectively. Also in the city of Ashkhabad, 37.9% of the children could be placed in kindergartens. This pattern also holds true for Kirgiz SSR and for nurseries as well as kindergartens. (Dodge, 1966: 80,85) It is notable that in 1959 about 50% of Ashkhabad's population were of Russian nationality; 30% were native. (Bondarskaia, 1970: 174) Comparing Turkmen and Kirgiz SSR's, Dodge (1966: 86) notes that overall the kindergarten facilities in the major urban areas are sufficient to accommodate about 40% of the estimated kindergarten age children. By contrast, rural facilities can accommodate only 5-10% of such children.

The figures on the distribution of child care facilities in rural and urban areas suggest that the expansion of child care facilities was being used to reconcile the work and family roles of urban women--most of whom were of Russian and other European nationalities. The rural areas, having less priority in Soviet development plans as well as less urgent need for child care

42

facilities, received much less aid. This is true in both European and non-European republics. In his discussion of child care in the USSR, Dodge (1966: 86) draws similar conclusions: ". . . in the large cities, where the government is particularly eager to attract women into the productive labor force, the percentage of children who can be accommodated is substantially larger than the average figures for the U.S.S.R. as a whole, or for urban areas as a whole, would suggest."

b. Family allowances and motherhood awards

Many of the family policies could not have been established with the non-European population in mind. As the statistics on divorce show, divorce has been a rarity in the non-European republics, especially in rural areas. It is also doubtful that much illegitimacy occurred since most non-European marry before age 20 (Urlanis, 1963: 38) and stable family life is customary. And it is unlikely that abortion and contraception policies were directed toward the non-European because, at least into the 1950s, there was no family planning practiced among non-European groups. (Sifman, 1968: 124-25) But due to their large families, non-Europeans have been, in proportion to their numbers, the most qualified to receive family allowances and motherhood awards.

There is apparently no data on recipients of family allowances by region or nationality. However, if the average size of families by region and nationality can be considered a gauge of who is qualified to receive allowances, the non-European population significantly exceeds most European groups. As the table below shows, in 1959 all of the non-European nationalities had an average family size of 4.5 or more--at least .5 family members more than any European nationality. Data for years since 1959, presented in chapter 3, show that the gap between European and non-European family size remains large.

Average Family Size[*] by Nationality in 1959

Nationality	Avg. Number Family Members
USSR	3.7
Tadzhik	5.2
Uzbek	5.0
Turkmen	5.0
Azerbaidshan	4.8
Armenian	4.7
Kazakh	4.6
Kirgiz	4.5
Georgian	4.0
Moldavian	3.9
Belorussian	3.7
Russian	3.6
Lithuanian	3.6
Ukrainian	3.5
Latvian	3.1
Estonian	3.0

(Dodge, 1966: 26)

[*]Total number of persons sharing one household or the same budget--see footnote 26

The non-European population also receives a disproportionate share of motherhood awards. In a study done by Heer and Bryden (1966), the republics receiving the largest proportion of awards for mothers with 10 or more children were, with the exception of (largely rural) Lithuania and Moldavia, non-European.

The five republics with the largest number of awards are only 9% of the total population; yet they received 27% of the awards. With the exception of Armenia, these republics are predominantly Moslem.

In summary, I have tried to show how Soviet family policies applied to the Soviet population, since this is important if we are to understand why particular policies were chosen or to which groups the policies were relevant.

Average Number of Awards to Mothers of 10 or
More Children by Republic: 1962-63
(per million total population)

Area	Avg. Number of Mothers Receiving Awards
USSR	18
Ukrainian SSR	8
Estonian SSR	9
Belorussian SSR	11
Latvian SSR	12
RSFSR	14
Georgian SSR	19
Lithuanian SSR	33
Moldavian SSR	38
Kazakh SSR	33
Uzbek SSR	39
Armenian SSR	46
Kirgiz SSR	52
Turkmen SSR	54
Tadzhik SSR	64
Azerbaidzhan SSR	82

(Heer and Bryden, 1966: 158)

In urban areas, especially where Europeans were a large part of the population, child care and maternity benefits, divorce and illegitimacy laws, abortion and contraception policies were most applicable in order to encourage fertility and female employment. These family policies had must less application in rural areas. On the other hand, family allowances and motherhood award recipients were far more likely to be rural than urban families. Understanding to whom different policies applied is important if we are to determine the effectiveness of the policies. The next step is to examine whether or not family policies succeeded in promoting fertility and female employment and the reasons for success or failure.

CHAPTER 3

FERTILITY AND FEMALE LABOR FORCE TRENDS AND

THE ROLE OF FAMILY POLICIES

Evaluating the effectiveness of Soviet family policies is a difficult task, as one might suspect. There are many variables affecting fertility and female employment, so that assigning a weight to family policies can hardly be done in any precise, quantitative manner. Also it is true that fertility and female employment trends affect each other as well as influence the direction of family policies. I have attempted to deal with these reciprocal influences. Obviously, as already mentioned, the family policies of 1944 were a response to demographic trends and to projected needs. Actual trends have also resulted in alterations of policies, such as the relegalization of abortion in 1955. Furthermore, since 1960, actual trends have substantially altered the Soviet conception of the aims of family policies as well as the policies themselves. (Post-1959 trends are discussed in chapter 4.)

Recognizing the problems of measuring the effectiveness of family policies, I have attempted to ascertain whether or not Soviet family policy was at all successful in encouraging fertility and female employment. In answering this question, I have looked at the fertility and female employment trends since 1959 in the USSR as a whole, in rural and urban areas, and among Europeans and non-Europeans. Then I have examined the main socio-economic forces affecting these trends--namely, modernization and changing consumption standards. Finally, I have considered the impact of the family policies on fertility and female employment in light of these socio-economic forces.

It will be seen from trends in Soviet postwar fertility and female labor force participation that family policy has had little success in meeting its goals. The most important reason Soviet policy has been largely ineffective is that both high fertility and high female employment are conflicting aims given the social realities facing Soviet families. For the urban, mostly European, population these social realities are the concomitants of the economic development and modernization of the USSR: rising expectations for consumption and a more comfortable standard of living. These expectations in the USSR have been frustrated by continuing material hardship and scarcities in the consumer sector. The result has been high female labor force participation but very low fertility levels. The rural European population, where development and modernization has lagged behind that of urban areas, has been characterized by traditionally active participation in the agricultural economy and also relatively high (although declining) fertility levels. Finally, in the rural non-European republics, where modernization has had the least impact and traditional cultures prevail, female labor force participation is relatively low but fertility is consistently high.

Modernization and Population Trends

Before discussing how modernization has affected fertility and labor force trends in the USSR, a consideration of the historical relationship between modernization and population trends is in order. In the West, modernization, in the form of industrial development, urbanization, literacy, and improved living standards greatly altered both cultural and demographic

47

patterns. One concern in this paper is the role of women in society. Modernization brings about a greater freedom for women outside the home including a greater participation of women in the economy. At the same time, modernization has been accompanied by declining fertility levels. Without exception, modern industrial countries have low fertility levels. Family sizes tend to be small and conscious regulation of births by couples is widely practiced.

The process by which fertility declines from high to low levels is referred to by demographers as the "demographic transition."[22] According to the demographic transition model, a population's mortality and fertility rates undergo changes at different stages of modernization. In pre-modern societies, fertility and mortality rates are both high and there is little practice of birth control. As modernization occurs, mortality rates tend to decline due to improved sanitation, food, and medical care. Fertility rates initially remain high but eventually begin to decline. In the next stage of the transition, the one characteristic of modern societies, mortality and fertility levels are both low and birth control is widespread.

Explaining why the demographic transition in fertility occurs has been more difficult than describing it. Although it is easy to see why mortality declines, since few people resist practices that prolong or save life, the reasons for fertility declines are less obvious. In fact, it is not unreasonable to expect parents to produce more children since more could be provided for in a modern, prosperous society. (In some cases this has occurred, but usually temporarily.)

Most theories attempting to account for declining fertility in modernizing societies employ what is essentially an economic model based on the concept of "utility."[23] Utility refers to the value of a good, service, or activity. Children can be regarded, in a sense, as a "good" with certain utility or value within a family or a society. In a pre-modern society, for example, children are valued as additional workers, as a source of old-age security, or as socially prestigious. Industrialization and modernization change the utility of children. As upward mobility, living standards, and opportunities expand, other goods or desirables compete with children. For one, children lose their economic value and, with old-age pensions, their value as providers to aged parents. As infant mortality and childhood mortality decline, the need for a large family, to ensure that some will survive to maturity, become less important. Also other status symbols such as homes, education, and luxury goods or leisure begin to outweigh children. Thus families begin to have fewer children. A large family becomes increasingly burdensome as aspirations increase.

This pattern has prevailed in all modern societies. Those with high aspirations for the benefits of a modern society (either for themselves or their children) are the first to reduce fertility and to regulate their family size. As William Petersen (1969: 505) observes, "The modern small-family system originated among persons rising in the social scale. Not only can one move further and faster with fewer dependents, but in an upwardly mobile family aspirations are typically higher than any income can satisfy. . . ."

Essentially then, fertility control occurs among those groups who perceive the possibility of social and economic advancement. This, in turn, depends on exposure to new possibilities as well as a social climate in which the new possibilities are viewed positively by one's reference groups. It is not surprising that fertility declines are closely associated with urbanization,

49

education, and social class (e.g., occupation and income). It is typically rural or lower class groups, the last to experience the new opportunities, who are the last to limit their family size.

The Demographic Transition in the USSR

In the USSR the course of the demographic transition has been similar to that of other modern societies. As economic development and modernization have spread, so has lower fertility. The modern stage of the transition (low mortality and fertility) has been reached only in the postwar years, particularly since the 1960s. Vital rates for the USSR since 1913 give the changes that have occurred.

USSR Vital Rates: 1913-70
(per 1000 population)

Year	Births	Deaths	Year	Births	Deaths
1913	45.5	29.1	1940	31.2	18.0
1923*	42.2	22.9	1950	26.7	9.7
1928*	42.1	18.1	1955	25.7	8.2
1930	39.2	20.4	1960	24.9	7.1
1935	28.6	16.3	1965	18.4	7.3
			1970	17.4	8.2

*Only for European part of the USSR

(Years 1923-35 from Kulischer, 1948: 80; other years from TsSU, 1968: 12 and Vestnik statistiki, No. 12, 1973: 73)

In 1913 the Russian population was clearly in the pre-modern stage of demographic development. Birth and death rates were very high. Significant declines in fertility only began to occur around 1930, a period of intense social upheaval in the USSR caused by forced collectivization and industrialization. Before World War II, fertility rates were still high but significantly lower than in 1913.

Despite the tremendous losses of young men of childbearing age during

50

World War II, fertility rates into the 1950s were still moderately high. The birth rate after World War II would have been higher except for the unbalanced sex ratio. As late as 1959, 14 years after the war ended, there were over 20 million more females than males in the population. There were more females in all age groups over 19.

It is easy to see how the sex ratio would affect the marriage chances of women and hence fertility. After 1960 the birth rate began to drop precipitously. Part of the drop was due to the small cohort of World War II entering childbearing age; the sex ratio plays a smaller role. By 1970 there were almost as many males as females in the 20-39 age group, the age at which most children are born. At ages 20-24 there were more males than females.

Sex Ratio: 1959 and 1970
(Men and women per 1000
population)

Ages	1959		1970	
	Men	Women	Men	Women
15-19	501	499	510	490
20-24	494	506	504	496
25-29	490	510	495	505
30-34	453	547	492	508
35-39	391	609	491	509
40-44	384	616	461	539
45-49	384	616	387	613
All Ages (15-49) (men per 1000 women)	819		855	

(TsSU, Vol. 2, 1973: 9-11, 14)

The decline in fertility is also indicated by the gross and net reproduction rates (GRR and NRR) since 1938. These rates are hypothetical, indicating the number of female births that would occur per 1000 women during their reproductive years if the level of fertility of a given years were maintained. The NRR takes into account mortality that would occur among the women; thus this rate is typically lower than the GRR, which measures only fertility. A GRR or NRR of 1.0 or less would indicate that the population would eventually no longer grow or would even begin to decline in numbers.[24] By 1964-65 the population of the USSR was at the point that current levels of reproduction, if continued, would result in very low population growth.

Gross and Net Reproduction Rates: 1938-72

Years	GRR	NRR	Years	GRR	NRR
1938/39	2.10	1.40	1964/65	1.19	1.13
1959		1.30	1970/71	1.20	1.15
1960/61	1.36	1.27	1971/72	1.20	1.15
1962/63	1.26	1.18			

(Eason, 1968: 217; Vestnik statistiki, No. 12, 1973: 75)

a. Rural-urban fertility

More important for my purposes than general fertility trends are rural-urban differentials. Before the war, rural and urban crude birth rates were almost the same. After the war, the gap between rural and urban fertility began to widen, as reflected in the crude birth rates.

Rural-Urban Crude Birth Rates: 1940-70
(births per 1000 population)

Year	Urban	Rural
1940	30.5	31.5
1950	26.0	27.1
1955	23.5	27.4
1960	21.9	27.8
1965	16.1	21.1
1970	16.4	18.7

(Volkov, 1972: 111)

The extent of the difference in rural-urban fertility is not reflected in the crude rates, which are based on total population regardless of age or sex. The urban population has proportionately more young people of childbearing age than the rural population due to heavy immigration of young people after the war. According to migration expert Perevedentsev (in Kvasha, 1974: 38), about 2/3 of urban migrants are 15-29 years of age.

The impact of age composition can be seen from the number of individual 20-29 in the rural and urban areas. In 1959 there were 20.4 million young people between these ages in the urban areas and 18.1 million in the rural areas. The difference is more striking in 1970--there are 20.7 million in cities compared to only 10.1 million in the rural areas. (TsSU, Vol. 2, 1972: 14-15) Thus the probability of getting married and having children has been much more favorable in urban than rural areas.

Indeed, urban women are far more likely to be married than rural women. In a study done by Dar'skii (1968), the percentage of urban women never married by age 50 from 1949-59 was far less than for rural women. Controlling for regional fertility differences (high--crude birth rate [CBR] above 30, moderate--CBR of 20-30, or low--CBR below 20), Dar'skii found that in the low and moderate fertility regions (all European), less than 5% of urban women had never been married; from about 15-22% of rural women had never been married. In high fertility regions (non-Europeans), less than 4% of both urban and rural women had never been married. (Dar'skii, 1968: 100)

Another factor of equal importance to rural-urban fertility is the sex ratio. (See table below) In urban areas the sex ratio is more equal, promoting higher marriage and fertility rates.[25] In 1959 the urban sex ratio (males per 1000 females) was 825; the rural ratio was 814. By 1970 the rural ratio was more equal, but the gap was greater between the rural and urban sex ratios--843 to 864, respectively. Census data for 1959 and 1970 also show that in 1959, after the ages of 20-24, the urban sex ratio was more equal than

53

the rural sex ratio. In 1970, for ages 20-29 (the peak childbearing years), the sex ratio in the urban areas is almost equal but still disproportionate in rural areas.

Urban and Rural Sex Ratios: 1959 and 1970
(men and women per 1000 population)

Ages	Urban				Rural			
	M	F	M	F	M	F	M	F
15-19	494	506	505	495	509	491	520	480
20-24	486	514	502	498	504	496	509	491
25-29	494	506	500	500	486	514	486	514
30-34	458	542	492	508	448	552	492	508
35-39	390	610	490	510	392	608	491	509
40-44	402	598	467	533	363	637	451	549
45-49	405	595	387	613	362	638	387	613

All Ages (men per 1000 women)	1959	1970
Urban	825	864
Rural	814	843

(TsSU, Vol. 2, 1973: 9-11, 14)

The sex ratio in 1970 has some bearing on the crude birth rates for that year. In urban areas one would have expected the crude birth rate to be higher, especially since the 20-29 age group is composed of the large cohort of postwar babies. The low rural birth rate has been affected substantially by the unfavorable sex ratio that exists.

A more sensitive measure of rural-urban fertility differences than the crude birth rate is based on births to married women of childbearing age. R. I. Sifman, a Soviet demographer, has compiled completed cohort fertility data for women in the USSR as a whole and for rural and urban women. His figures show the number of children born per 1000 women during a given five-year period. According to Sifman's calculations, Soviet women born since 1889 and before have in general been increasingly restricting the number of children they have (for whatever reason). Dramatic changes in family size, however,

54

appear mainly to have begun only during the Soviet period with women born between 1900-04. More than half of all Soviet women born in 1910-14 had no more than three children, while only about one-third of women born twenty years earlier had three or fewer children. The difference between rural and urban women is also considerable. Although both rural and urban women born since 1900 show marked declines in family size compared to women born earlier, urban women have far fewer children than rural women. Over 2/3 of the 1910-14 urban cohort had three or fewer children compared to less than half of rural women. Moreover, far more rural than urban women have had the large families that would make them eligible for family allowances and motherhood awards. Less than 20% of the 1910-14 urban cohort (these women were the last cohort to reach the end of their childbearing years in 1959 when Sifman's data were compiled) had 5 or more children compared to over 36% of rural women of this cohort. (Sifman, 1970: 150)

Recent data on age-specific fertility and the general fertility rate (GFR) (births in a given year per 1000 women 15-49) are another good indication that differences in rural-urban fertility are large despite crude birth rates. The 1971-72 GFR for urban women was far lower than the rural rate. And age-specific rates show that regardless of age group, rural women still have significantly more births than urban women.

The average size of the rural family is also, as one might suspect, considerably larger than the urban family. In 1959 the average rural family was composed of 3.9 members; in 1970 the figure was 4.0. The urban family had 3.5 members in both 1959 and 1970. The percentage of large families has declined for urban families but has risen for rural families. Urban families with 5 or more members has declined from 21% in 1959 to 18% in 1970. The

55

rural figure is 31% in 1959 and 33% in 1970--an increase.

General Fertility and Age-Specific
Fertility Rates: 1971-72
(births per 1000 women)

Ages	Total	Urban	Rural
15-49 (GFR)	67.2	57.9	83.5
up to 20	32.4	30.2	36.1
20-24	173.9	150.5	231.9
25-29	137.1	116.7	179.2
30-34	84.3	66.0	118.6
35-39	49.4	31.8	76.8
40-44	14.6	6.8	26.3
45-49	2.0	.7	4.1

(Vestnik statistiki, No. 12, 1973: 75)

Size of Urban and Rural Families:
1959 and 1970

	Urban		Rural	
Per 1000 families, those with	1959	1970	1959	1970
2 persons	271	252	249	257
3	289	303	233	205
4	230	266	205	206
5	121	111	147	146
6	53	40	89	86
7	21	14	43	46
8	9	7	20	27
9	4	4	8	15
10+	2	3	6	12

(Vestnik statistiki, No. 11, 1973: 75)

In Belova and Dar'skii's 1969 study (Belova, 1975: 127), significant differences were found in ideal and expected family size (i.e., number of children) between rural and urban women. On the average, rural women found 3.47 children to be ideal, but expected 3.32 children. Urban women found 2.74 children the ideal number; they expected only 2.19 children--more than one child less than rural women.

As the data show, in sum, both rural and urban fertility have been declining in the USSR, but rural rates have not declined as much as crude birth rates would suggest. And rural fertility is still significantly higher than urban fertility. Some of the declines in both rural and urban areas are due to such demographic factors as age and sex composition; but, especially among urban families, the major factors are socio-economic.

b. Social class and fertility

Although the urban population is more modern and has lower fertility than the rural population, the influence of modernization on fertility is also seen within the urban population itself and deserves some mention. Differences in fertility are found with such social class variables as occupation, education, and income. This is consistent with the expectations of the utility model discussed earlier. It must be admitted, however, that data on social class are less abundant than for rural-urban residence or nationality. For one, Soviet statistics only recognize three social, actually occupational, classes: farm workers, industrial workers, and service workers (white collar). Another problem is that apparently Soviet researchers have not until recently begun to investigate the relationship between social class variables and fertility. Another problem is that even the data available does not differentiate middle from high status groups within occupational classes. This limits the value of the data in showing actual social class differences. At any rate, however vague and inadequate for comparative purposes the Soviet class distinctions may appear to be, they do allow for some social status comparisons. Service workers enjoy more prestige, if not always wages, than manual workers and their life styles and aspirations are different. (Cf. Geiger, 1968: 210; Sorlin, 1968: 234) Farm workers are the lowest of the

57

three groups in both prestige and income.

Occupational differences in the number of children in 1962 were provided by B. Urlanis (1963: 66) in his book on the Soviet population. According to his data, 28% of farm worker families had three or more children compared to 15% of manual workers and only 9% of service workers. Only 1% of service workers had more than 3 children (the minimum to receive any monthly family allowances).

Number of Children by Social Class: 1962
(in percent)

Families with	Farm	Workers	Service Workers
1 child	40	46	50
2 children	32	39	41
3	19	12	8
4+	9	3	1

(Urlanis, 1963: 66)

Belova and Dar'skii's 1969 study of working women in Moscow also points to substantial social class differences in fertility. Taking age into account, manual workers in every age category expected more children than service workers. Although expected children are not the same as actual children, the widespread use and availability of abortion in Moscow would make it fairly easy for women to have the number of children they choose.

In the same study, income and education were also examined as variables in expected number of children. An inverse relationship existed in both cases; the higher the education or income, the fewer children expected.

Data from the 1970 census also confirm the relationship between social class and fertility. Service workers, urban or rural, have lower fertility (based on number of children) than industrial workers or farm workers, workers

Expected Number of Children by Age of Women

Age of Women	Average Expected Number of Children	
	Workers	Service Workers
Up to 25	2.00	1.64
25-29	1.89	1.57
30-34	1.80	1.53
35-39	1.86	1.58
Average	1.86	1.57

(Belova and Dar'skii, 1972: 119)

Expected Number of Children by Education of Women

Education of Women	Average Number of Children Expected
Higher and Unfinished Higher	1.54
Middle General and Specialist	1.63
Uncompleted Middle	1.81
Elementary or Less	1.90

Expected Number of Children by Income of Women

Per Capita Monthly Income of Women (rubles)	Average Number of Children Expected
Up to 50.0	2.22
50.0--74.9	1.83
75.0--99.9	1.54
100.0 and over	1.47

(Belova and Dar'skii, 1972: 116, 118)

in industry have lower fertility than farm workers. Interestingly, urban industrial workers have even lower fertility than rural service workers. This may reflect a standardization in family and other values in urban areas (see the discussion on cultural homogenization below) and a continuation of higher fertility norms in rural areas that affect all occupational groups.

Number of Children by Occupational Class
and Rural-Urban Residence: 1970
(children per 1000 mothers)

	Total	Urban	Rural
Industrial Workers	1978	1774	2377
Service Workers	1610	1537	1918
Farm Workers	2415		2437

(TsSU, Vol. 7, 1974: 444)

The same relationship found with occupation also exists between educa-tion and the number of children. The higher the education, the smaller the number of children for both urban and rural women. However, as with occupa-tion, urban women in all but the lowest educational category, have fewer children than rural women of all educational levels.

Social class findings suggest that the problems as well as the oppor-tunities of urban life influence all groups in the city and bring about a lowering of fertility. In rural areas, fertility remains higher than in the city regardless of social class.

c. European and non-European fertility

The differences observed between rural and urban fertility since World War II are in part a nationality difference. Europeans comprise most of the urban, industrial, and modern portion of the USSR and have the lowest ferti-lity. Most non-Europeans have been rural and they traditionally have very high fertility. While both groups have undergone crude birth rate declines from 1961 to 1972, none of the non-European republics falls in the low fertility range (CBR below 20), whereas almost all European republics are within this range. In 1972 Moldavia is the one exception among European republics--with a crude birth rate of 20.6, just above the low fertility group.

60

Most non-European republics are still in the high fertility group and have
CBR's over 30.

Crude Birth Rates by Republic: 1961 and 1972
(births per 1000 population)

CBR	1959	1970
15-19.9	Ukraine, Latvia, Estonia	RSFSR, Ukraine, Lithuania, Latvia, Estonia, Georgia, Belorussia
20-24.9	RSFSR, Lithuania, Georgia, Belorussia	Moldavia, Armenia, Kazakh
25-29.9	Moldavia	Azerbaidzhan
30-34.9	Tadzhik	Uzbek, Turkmen, Kirgiz
35-39.9	Kazakh, Uzbek, Kirgiz, Armenia	Tadzhik
40-44.9	Azerbaidzhan, Turkmen	

(Urlanis, 1963: 37; Vestnik statistiki, No. 12, 1973: 76-79)

Size of family by republic and nationality further indicates the wide
disparity between European and non-European fertility. European fertility,
both urban and rural, is typically lower than non-European fertility in urban
areas. This is even more true in 1970 than in 1959, according to census
figures. While European republics register little change or even declines in
family size, non-European republics have, in most cases, shown surprising
increases in family size. The increases occur mainly in the number of very
large families of 7 or more members. (Vestnik statistiki, No. 11, 1973: 76-77)
The large increases in family size are occurring at the same time that crude
birth rates declined. Among European republics in both 1959 and 1970, only
in Georgia was the average family size (and only in rural areas) as high as 4.
During this same period, most European republics had average family sizes
closer to 5 members, and rural rates were as high as 6.

Average Family Size[26] by Republic and Rural-Urban
Residence: 1959 and 1970

	Average Size Family			Average Size Family	
	1959	1970		1959	1970
USSR	3.7	3.7	Ukraine	3.5	3.4
Urban	3.5	3.5	Urban	3.4	3.3
Rural	3.9	4.0	Rural	3.7	3.6
RSFSR	3.6	3.5	Uzbek	4.6	5.3
Urban	3.5	3.4	Urban	4.1	4.5
Rural	3.8	3.8	Rural	4.8	5.8
Lithuania	3.6	3.4	Azerbaidzhan	4.5	5.1
Urban	3.4	3.4	Urban	4.1	4.5
Rural	3.7	3.5	Rural	4.9	5.7
Latvia	3.2	3.2	Armenia	4.8	5.0
Urban	3.1	3.2	Urban	4.5	4.7
Rural	3.2	3.2	Rural	5.1	5.5
Estonia	3.1	3.1	Kirgiz	4.2	4.0
Urban	3.1	3.2	Urban	3.9	4.0
Rural	3.1	3.1	Rural	4.4	5.1
Georgia	4.0	4.1	Tadzhik	4.7	5.4
Urban	3.7	3.8	Urban	4.1	4.5
Rural	4.2	4.3	Rural	5.1	6.0
Belorussia	3.7	3.6	Turkmen	4.5	5.2
Urban	3.5	3.5	Urban	4.0	4.6
Rural	3.8	3.7	Rural	5.0	6.0
Moldavia	3.8	3.8	Kazakh	4.1	4.3
Urban	3.5	3.4	Urban	3.9	3.9
Rural	3.9	3.9	Rural	4.3	4.8

(TsSU, Vol. 7, 1974: 234-37)

Another indication of the wide difference between European and non-European fertility is provided by Belova (1975: 66) in her study of nationality differences in ideal and expected number of children among married women. The average ideal number of children was given as 2.68 by European women, but as 6.05 by non-European women. European women actually expected to have only 2.16 children, whereas non-European women expected to have even more children than their ideal number--6.24.

When family size by nationality rather than republic is examined, larger differences are shown. The impact of Russian immigration, in particular, has been to significantly lower non-European republic family sizes, since Russians have much lower fertility than the native populations. It is notable that even in urban areas of non-European republics, the native population shows traditionally large family sizes; little difference, in fact, is shown between urban and rural areas.

Family Size by Russian and Native Nationality in
non-European Republics: 1970

Republic	Russian	Native	Republic	Russian	Native
Uzbek	3.4	5.9	Tadzhik	3.4	6.1
Urban	3.4	5.8	Urban	3.4	5.9
Rural	3.5	6.0	Rural	3.4	6.2
Kazakh	3.6	5.5	Armenia	3.5	5.0
Urban	3.5	5.4	Urban	3.4	4.7
Rural	3.9	5.5	Rural	3.7	5.4
Azerbaidzhan	3.4	5.6	Turkmen	3.3	6.0
Urban	3.3	5.1	Urban	3.3	5.9
Rural	3.8	5.9	Rural	3.4	6.0
Kirgiz	3.5	5.5			
Urban	3.5	5.1			
Rural	3.6	5.6			

(TsSU, Vol. 7, 1974: 284-303)

The increase in family size in non-European republics since 1959 is attributed to continued high fertility along with declining mortality, especially infant mortality. Recent crude birth rate declines do not represent actual declines in fertility among non-European nationalities. For one, the crude rates appear to be affected by age composition. There has been a substantial decline since 1959 in the number of young people in rural areas where fertility has been the highest. Age composition does not, however, necessarily affect family size. Another factor in recent crude birth rate declines is the proportion of the population that is European. The percent of the population urban is also related to lower birth rates.

For example, in the non-European republics of Azerbaidzhan, Armenia, and Kazakhstan, the crude birth rates in 1972 ranged from 22.5-25.6 (moderate).

63

Of all the non-European republics, Azerbaidzhan and Armenia both show the greatest declines since 1959 in the number of young people 20-29 among the rural population--close to 50% in both cases. There is also little growth or even some decline in the urban population for this age group. Undoubtedly, this decline in the number of young people would lower the birth rate, since ages 20-29 are peak childbearing years. In Kazakhstan, the rural 20-29 age group has also declined significantly, though not as sharply as in Azerbaidzhan or Armenia. The fact that over 50% of the population of Kazakhstan is European may explain much of the decline in birth rates. Russians alone are 42% of the total population of Kazakhstan and 50% of the urban population. Notably, all three republics having the lowest non-European crude birth rates are the most urban of the non-European republics--50% or more.

On the other hand, in the non-European republics with the highest fertility (CBR's over 30)--Tadzhik, Turkmen, Uzbek, and Kirgiz republics--the 20-29 age group has declined less in the rural areas. And, except for Turkmen, over 62% of their populations are rural. Europeans are less than 20% of the population in these republics with the exception of Kirgiz--about 1/3 are Europeans.

Urbanization and European nationality are closely related to lower fertility in all republics of the USSR, not just the non-European republics. According to 1970 census figures, in all republics where the crude birth rate is in the 20s or below, the population is 50% or more urban or European or both. This is true even when there are large rural populations as well (e.g., the republics of Moldavia and Belorussia are largely rural, yet have low crude birth rates). If the majority of the population is urban or European, fertility is moderate or low. The correlation between urbanization, European

Demographic Factors in non-European Fertility:
Crude Birth Rates (births per 1000 popula-
tion), Percent Urban, Percent of Popu-
lation Russian, and Changes in
Percent of Rural Population
Aged 20-24 and 25-29
From 1959 to 1970

Republic	1971 CBR	1970 % Urban	1970 % Russian in Population	Rural Population 1970 as % of 1959	
				Ages 20-24	Ages 25-29
Uzbek	34.5	37	12.5	82	78
Kazakh	23.5	50	42.4	67	89
Azerbaidzhan	27.7	50	10.0	51	53
Kirgiz	31.6	37	29.2	79	70
Tadzhik	36.8	37	11.9	75	74
Armenia	22.6	59	2.7	50	50
Turkmen	33.9	48	14.5	92	80

(TsSU, Vol. 1 1972: 8; Vol. 2, 1972: 12-75; Vol. 4, 1973: 14-15, 202-316;
Vestnik statistiki, No. 12, 1973; 76-79)

nationality, and fertility reflects the process of modernization in the USSR.

Sex and age composition differences also exist between Europeans and
non-European republics and exert some influence on fertility differences. In
the European republics, for total population and rural or urban areas, the sex
ratio is below 900 (males per 1000 females) in every case. In the non-European
republics the sex ratio is above 900 in all cases. The sex ratio is thus more
favorable to fertility in non-European republics. Although the urban population of most republics is increasing; rural populations are declining in numbers, especially in younger ages (reflecting both lower fertility during the
1940s and out-migration). The European republics have been even harder hit.
In the European rural areas, the 20-29 age group has in most cases declined by
30% or more since 1959. Of the non-European republics, only Kazakhstan,
Azerbaidzhan, and Armenia--show such large deficits. (TsSU, Vol. 2, 1972:5-75)
It should be added that in most republics, the urban population 20-29 has

grown since 1959.

Age and Sex Composition by Republic: 1970

Republic	Sex Ratio[*]	1970 as % of 1959 Ages 20-24	1970 as % of 1959 Ages 25-29
RSFSR	838	51	45
Ukraine	825	52	71
Belorussia	851	46	47
Uzbek	949	82	78
Kazakh	928	67	89
Georgia	887	61	67
Azerbaidzhan	943	51	53
Lithuania	884	60	70
Moldavia	872	65	81
Latvia	842	67	89
Kirgiz	915	79	70
Tadzhik	968	75	74
Armenia	955	50	50
Turkmen	970	92	80
Estonia	843	79	83

(*men per 1000 women)

(TsSU, Vol. 2, 1972: 5-75)

As can be seen from the above discussion, recent declines in non-European birth rates reflect such factors as age composition and sex ratio imbalance, especially in rural areas. Urbanization and the proportion of the population that is European are other important influences. There does not appear to be a trend toward lower fertility or smaller family size among the native populations of these republics.

Soviet empirical studies also confirm the pervasively high fertility among the non-Europeans. L. Altyeva's study of rural married women in Turkmen reveals that even among your women, high fertility values prevail. In the study, 600 women up to 55 years old in two collective farms in the Ashkhabad region were interviewed. Altyeva (1973: 74) found that 52.3% of families had 7 or more members. The average number of children per family was four.

When asked their ideal number of children, only a few women (those with secondary education or better) gave a definite number or thought that one should even plan one's family size. Most responded with answers like "the more the better" or "whatever nature brought was fine." Few women practiced birth control; the women who did were the most educated. Even the women who did believe in planning their family size considered that 4-5 children was the ideal. This number is considerably larger than the 1, 2, or 3 children considered ideal by European women.

The consumption values that have become prevalent among the European population were found not to have appreciably affected the Turkmen women. Among these women, education and material prosperity did not result in lower fertility. (Altyeva, 1973: 82) Apparently, the social pressures and traditions supportive of large families remain operative in the rural areas.[27]

Other research has been done on the differences in fertility values between Europeans and non-Europeans. Belova and Dar'skii (1972: 102) studied ideal and expected family size among women in the republics. With the exception of Georgia, both the ideal and expected family size is at least half a child more in the non-European republics. Furthermore, the non-European women reported that their husbands wanted even more children than they did; the opposite was true among women in the European republics. Although the differences between wife and husband are small in most cases, the fact that the relationship exists in every instance is curious. A speculative explanation for the relationship may be that in the traditional non-European republics, the prestige and economic value of children to the father is perceived by the wife and results in her higher estimation of the father's desire for children.[28] In the more modern European republics, the social and economic costs of children to the father, who is usually the primary bread winner, tend to result in the wife's lower estimation of the number of children her husband would want compared to her own desires.

Number of Children Reported by Women as Ideal,
Expected, and Desired by Husband in USSR
Republics (average number of children)

	Ideal	Expected	Desired by Husband
USSR	2.89	2.42	2.85
Latvia	2.60	2.11	2.46
Ukraine	2.63	2.07	2.52
RSFSR	2.69	2.21	2.60
Estonia	2.74	2.29	2.51
Moldavia	2.74	2.25	2.70
Lithuania	2.75	2.20	2.66
Belorussia	2.93	2.41	2.83
Kazakh	3.38	3.19	3.56
Kirgiz	3.94	3.72	4.35
Georgia	3.95	2.88	3.90
Armenia	4.10	3.42	4.44
Turkmen	4.10	3.79	4.34
Tadzhik	4.18	4.08	4.62
Azerbaidzhan	4.52	4.25	4.70
Uzbek	4.55	4.31	4.84

(Belova and Dar'skii, 1972: 102)

It is interesting that in every republic women expect fewer children than they think is ideal. This suggests that non-Europeans as well as Europeans may be facing pressures to lower fertility. However, data supplied by Belova (1975: 66) on nationality differences within the Central Asian republics indicate that it is European women in these republics who expect fewer children than their ideal number. Non-European women actually expect more than their ideal numbers. The ideal and expected number of children for non-European women in these republics is 6.62 and 6.75. The corresponding figures for European women are 3.18 and 2.74.

Female Labor Force Participation

Trends in female labor force participation closely parallel developments in fertility. As is true of other industrialized, modern societies, a large percentage of Soviet women work outside the home. There are, however, important differences between Western and Soviet female employment trends. These differences have a bearing on family policy. One difference is that Soviet ideology strongly advocates female employment and equality of opportunity for women outside the home. In fact, women who do not work or who are "just housewives" are often considered "parasites." Thus there is a great deal of social pressure for women to get jobs. Another difference is the uniquely high percentage of Soviet women employed and the fact that so many remain employed after they begin to have children. In other developed countries, women tend to withdraw from the labor force during their childrearing years. According to Dodge (1966: 239-40), in the early 1960s about 70% of working-age women in the USSR were employed. This figure was twice the rate in the USA. And in the age group 20-39 about 80% of women were employed. In 1970 about 86% of Soviet women aged 16-54 were employed. (TsSU, Vol. 2, 1972: 12-13; Vol. 6, 1973: 165)

Rural-urban and Nationality Differences in Female Labor Force Participation

Level of modernization is closely connected to the rate of female employment for various population groups in the USSR. Those sectors of the population that are more urban, industrial, and undergoing changing standards of living show the greatest participation rates. As might be expected, urban women have higher rates of employment than rural women and European women are more likely to work than their non-European counterparts.

The rates of female employment are given in 1959 and 1970 Soviet census figures. Rural-urban and nationality differences also are provided. There are notable differences in employment for these groups.

Percent of Women Employed by Republic:
1959 and 1970

Republic	1959 % Employed	1970 % Employed	Republic	1959 % Employed	1970 % Employed
USSR	41.5	44.0	Georgia	38.8	40.8
Urban	39.4	48.7	Urban	31.7	41.1
Rural	43.4	38.1	Rural	44.2	40.5
RSFSR	41.9	46.0	Uzbek	33.9	33.5
Urban	42.1	50.8	Urban	28.3	36.4
Rural	41.8	38.3	Rural	36.7	31.9
Ukraine	43.6	45.6	Kazakh	30.4	38.0
Urban	36.8	48.4	Urban	30.6	43.4
Rural	49.3	42.4	Rural	30.2	32.6
Belorussia	48.6	45.1	Azerbaidzhan	34.5	30.0
Urban	41.0	51.9	Urban	27.4	32.4
Rural	51.9	40.1	Rural	41.0	27.5
Lithuania	42.6	44.9	Kirgiz	34.0	35.5
Urban	37.2	51.1	Urban	30.4	41.2
Rural	46.0	38.8	Rural	35.8	32.1
Moldavia	51.1	48.4	Tadzhik	35.0	30.8
Urban	36.7	50.5	Urban	30.1	36.0
Rural	55.3	47.4	Rural	37.5	27.6
Latvia	44.3	49.4	Armenia	32.0	35.5
Urban	43.0	54.7	Urban	26.1	37.2
Rural	45.9	40.7	Rural	37.8	33.2
Estonia	44.9	49.2	Turkmen	32.2	33.4
Urban	44.6	54.4	Urban	29.0	35.0
Rural	45.5	39.4	Rural	35.1	31.9

(TsSU, Vol. 5, 1973: 154-61)

One of the most striking differences is that, without exception, European republics have markedly higher female employment than non-European republics. In 1959 the percentage of women working ranged from 38.8-51.1% in European republics compared to 30.4-35% of women in non-European republics. In 1970 the ranges are 40.8-49.4% and 30-38%, respectively.

Rural-urban employment differences also indicate important contrasts between European and non-European republics. In all republics in 1959, more rural than urban women were in the work force. This is due partly to the fact that many rural women work only part time during the agricultural season. Their inclusion in labor statistics overinflates the actual level of female work force participation. (Cf. Heer, 1968: 235-36) It should be remembered that Russian women have traditionally worked in agriculture; their high work rates more accurately reflect old cultural practices than modernization and expanded roles for women. European-non-European differences for both rural and urban women are still evident. Without exception, women in European republics are more likely to be employed.

In 1970 the rural-urban employment difference is reversed. Significantly more urban women work than rural women. One reason is the migration to urban areas of young women seeking work. Also, mainly in the European republics, many women who worked in 1959 are now retired or on pension. As in 1959, more European women work than non-Europeans. The proportion of women of working-age (16-54) has some bearing on the 1970 figures. In European republics, the number of working age women has plummeted in most rural areas by as much as 26% since 1959. This drop would explain much of the decline in the proportion of European women employed in rural areas. The non-European rural areas, by contrast, have grown in almost every instance; yet the proportion of women employed has declined since 1959. The non-European rural decline in female employment may be due to declining mortality levels that have increased the proportion of dependent females (children and older women), even though the number of working age women has increased. In the case of non-European urban employment, much of the increase may be due to the immigration of European migrants rather than employment of the native population.

71

Fertility and Female Employment

As discussed above, the evidence suggests that as modernization increases, fertility declines and female employment increases. This is not what Soviet planners had hoped. While it is true that female labor force participation was desired, the Soviets needed to insure future labor force needs by encouraging women to both work and have children. These goals were, unfortunately, incompatible. In fact, Soviet researchers are finding that the conflicting demands of work and home are closely related to lower fertility.

A 1959 study of female employment and fertility conducted by Vostrikova (in Berent, 1970: 190), revealed an inverse relationship between employment and the number of children urban women had. In addition, the number of children was smallest for women who had been active in the labor force the longest time. Women who had never worked tended to have more children, especially among women 44 or younger, than those who had been active in the work force. Interestingly, among collective farmers, Vostrikova found little difference in number of children between active and non-active women. This is consistent with the remarks made earlier about the traditional work role of rural women and the seasonal nature of their employment. Work and family have not been as incompatible for these women as for urban women; therefore, female employment is not a major factor in their fertility levels.

Findings similar to Vostrikova's are reported in more recent studies. Prokopet's 1968 study, mentioned by Soviet family sociologist, A. Kharchev (1971: 88), showed that working women regardless of age group had fewer children than non-working women. The figures for working women were even lower when rural women were excluded from the sample.

In another study, Zvidrin'sh (1970: 252), who studied married Latvian rural and urban women, found that employed women had fewer children than women who did not work.

Research on abortion, the major form of birth control in the USSR, also suggests that it is working women who are more likely to limit their family size to a small number of children. In general, it is mainly married women aged 26 and over who already have children who resort to abortion. Statistics for 1963 in Leningrad medical establishments, for example, show that 80% of abortions were performed on married women; 70% were on women 26 and over. These women simply did not want additional children. (Kurganov, 1968: 191-92) Although these statistics did not distinguish the abortions of working or non-working women, a study of medical abortions in RSFSR republic showed that the abortion rate for working women was over twice that of non-working women-- there were 105.5 abortions per 1000 working women compared to 41.5 for non-working women. (Sadvokasova, 1968: 213)

The widespread use of abortion among working women is shown in a 1966 study in Moscow. In this study, 78% of unwanted pregnancies among working women were aborted even if no children were in the family. If the woman had one child, 97% of unwanted pregnancies ended in abortion. All unwanted pregnancies were aborted if there were already 2 or more children in the family. (Belova and Dar'skii, 1968: 33) Data on the prevalence of abortion, to be discussed below, reveal that a large proportion of pregnancies are unwanted.

The falling birth rate, especially in the urban areas, has caused much alarm among Soviet family experts. The incompatibilities between the worker and mother roles has been the subject of considerable study. A leading family researcher, A. Kharchev (1969: 33), refers to this problem as "one of the main causes of the declining birth rate." A common explanation for worker-mother role conflict is that, despite the fact that women have gained the "freedom" to be full time workers, they still find themselves bearing most of the traditional burdens of housework and childrearing. According to Iankova (1970: 78-79), most time budget studies have found that women spend almost four hours per day at homemaking. This is often in addition to a full work day. Husbands usually help little with housework and, since most families don't live with their parents anymore, there is no one to help the women. Also, despite Soviet policies designed to lighten the woman's domestic burdens, social services and labor-saving devices are inadequate even in large cities.

The extent of the domestic burden borne by working women was the subject of an investigation by Kharchev and Golod (1971: 70-74). Between 1965-68, over 1200 industrial workers (all married women) in Leningrad and Kostroma were interviewed. The object of the study was to determine which members of the family helped with housework. Over 80% of the women responded that they alone did the housework. In younger families the husband sometimes helped with the dishes and tidying up. This was rarely true in older families, however.

Some mention is relevant here on the traditional role of the grandmother ("babushka") in the Russian family. The husband or wife's mother often lived with the family and was a major source of domestic help, thus lightening the household burdens of Russian women. This was due not only to a tradition of extended families, but also to the fact that so many Soviet women were widows. Having a grandmother's help made it much easier for Soviet women to work outside the home.

In more recent years, older women are no longer as dependent on their children as before since they either work or receive pensions. In a 1966 study by Belova and Dar'skii (1972: 121), 1/3 of older women reported that they did not help with housework or raising children.

The decline in the number of older women helping in their children's homes has had an effect on fertility among younger women. Even the birth of a second child appears to be influenced by whether or not the grandmother's help is available. Belova and Dar'skii's (1972: 121) findings were that among one-child mothers under 35 with no one to help with housework and childrearing, only 50% wanted a second child. Among those who had the help of their mother-in-law, 55% wanted a second child; 63% wanted a second child if they had their own mother's help. Women who had to depend on other relatives to help bring up their children were least inclined to have a second child--only 23% intended to do so.

The Growth of Consumption after World War II

Although there seems to be a close relationship between female employ-ment and declining fertility, the evidence suggests that the relationship is indirect; i.e., the same factors contributing to low fertility may also be responsible for high rates of female employment. The key to the relationship between fertility and employment is found in the utility model discussed above. To reiterate, modernization brings about a change in consumption habits and goals. If a higher standard of living is to be acquired or maintained, families often must limit the number of children they have. And, in the case of the USSR, the women must work. Until recent years, these changes have affected mainly the urban, European population; but as modernization and rising consumption standards become more diffused, population trends in other areas of the country are being affected.

a. Consumption, fertility, and female employment

The relationship between fertility, female employment, and consumption is increasingly acknowledged in recent Soviet and Western discussions of the Soviet birth rate problem. In studies of regional fertility trends, Mazur (1967A: 45; 1968: 331-33) noted that the relationship between female employment and low fertility could be due to the fact that women work because of the husband's low wages. Level of modernization is also closely connected to differential fertility among working and non-working women. Mazur also points out that consumption demands affect fertility--but mainly among the urban population.

If originally material hardship was responsible for high female employment and declining fertility, this seems to be far less important now that basic living levels have improved considerably, as will be seen shortly. As the utility model suggests, new "needs" and standards arise as modernization and new opportunities develop. This conclusion is also reached by Berent (1970: 196-77): "If, in the earlier stages of the industrialization drive, the basic financial needs of the family often called for a contribution from its female members, in the later stages--when there had been a considerable improvement in living standards and in the supply of consumer goods and services--family aspirations of a more sophisticated type (for consumer durables, cooperative flats, foreign travel, etc.) began to exert some influence, maintaining a high employment demand among female household members." The same process results not only in high rates of female employment, but also declining fertility. In a paper in the Soviet journal, Voprosy ekonomiki, female employment and the birth rate were discussed. The author pointed out that although some women work out of necessity, they also work as a matter of custom. Many women who work find it difficult to take care of children, or they find that their goals for a better life conflict with their desires to have children. (K., 1969: 61-64)

Soviet demographer D. Valentei (1971: 329, 333-34), contends that employment of women does not directly affect fertility. Rather, employment gives rise to a growth in consumption and this is what affects fertility. Valentei extends this analysis to variables such as industrialization, urbanization, education, and increased cultural level--it is only by raising the level of consumption that these social factors appreciably affect fertility. And, in a position directly paralleling that of Western demographers using the utility model, Valentei notes that the demands for goods always move ahead of the possibility of satisfying them. But the demand for consumption proceeds at different rates among different groups and territories of the population. The regulation of births within the family is most pronounced among those groups with the greatest consumption demands in comparison with the ability to satisfy the demands. (The issue of consumption is also related to recent theoretical and policy discussions in the USSR. See chapter 4.)

Although both female employment and fertility are undoubtedly related to such demographic variables as sex ratio imbalances and age composition, these are typically temporary in their effects. Modernization, on the other hand, brings about far reaching and, so far historically, irreversible widespread participation of women in economic life and lower fertility.

A brief survey of postwar trends in consumption will show that the growth in wages, consumer goods, housing services, and popular aspirations for a

better life has been the most important influence on female employment and
fertility.

b. The rise in consumption

It is important to realize that modernization in the USSR before World
War II resulted in little lasting improvements in consumption and living
standards for the majority of people. During most of the Soviet period the
fruits of the Soviet worker's labor have been largely plowed back in the
economy rather than being used to promote consumption. When the standard of
living did increase, the areas primarily benefiting from modern improvements
have been overwhelmingly urban. Rural areas always have lagged behind,
especially those remote from urban areas. The areas least affected by modernization have been the traditional, non-European republics. The differences in
fertility and female employment in these areas have already been discussed,
and they correspond to the difference in level of modernization and consumption
demands.

Although the urban areas have been more modern and consumption higher
than elsewhere, until the 1950s material hardship was the rule for most of the
population including city dwellers. In the late 1940s, for example, household
consumption per capita was no greater than in the late 1920s. [29](Braverman,
1963: 72-73) It was only in the 1950s that goods such as vacuum cleaners,
TV's, washing machines, refrigerators, and cars began to appear. Even in the
1960s few people (mainly urbanites) possessed such items, and waiting lists
were long. (Hanson, 1968: 37-38) By the 1970s, according to Cohn (1973: 52),
58% of families had a washing machine, 38% had a refrigerator, but only 11%
owned a vacuum cleaner. Due to the extreme housing shortage, a construction
program was begun in 1956. Significant increases in social services such as

78

child care facilities and pension benefits also were instituted.

Due to such government efforts, the rate of growth of per capita consumption between 1950-1958 is estimated at 6-7% per year. From 1958-64, the rate of growth of consumption was around 4%, still a significant improvement. [30] (Hanson, 1968: 38-39) Also important is that the government itself began to promote and stimulate consumer appetites and to promise more goods and services. (Braverman, 1963: 82) [31]

The increases in the consumer sector of the economy were accompanied, beginning in 1953, by improved wages for both urban and rural workers. (Cf. Nove, 1969: 345-47) By December 1963, the minimum monthly wage for urban workers had been raised to 35 rubles. Most unskilled labor earned between 35-50 rubles working an 8-hour day, six days per week. Ten to fifteen percent of families were in this group. More than half of wage earners made 50-120 rubles per month. This included doctors, teachers, salesmen, bureaucrats, and 60% of skilled workers. About 20-25% of townspeople earned over 120 rubles. These included high officials, factory directors, professors, or scientists, and the best industrial workers. A salary of 300-400 rubles is not unusual for this group. (Sorlin, 1968: 233) (Rural wages will be discussed later.)

The Soviet wage scale is important to our understanding of both declining fertility and female employment, especially among urban European families. In 1965 the Soviet Scientific Research Institute of Labor (originally published in the Soviet journal, Voprosy ekonomiki) estimated that the minimum monthly income for material comfort for a family of four--parents plus a 13-year old boy and a 7-8-year old girl--was 206 rubles. (Soviet Review, 1970: 77) In terms of 1963 wages, we can see that over 3/4 of Soviet workers do not make enough money for material comfort! In 1967 the Research Institute adds, the average monthly wage for a worker or employee was 103.4 rubles or, including benefits from social consumption funds, 140.2 rubles. There were further increases in the average monthly wage in 1971 and 1973--to 122 and 135 rubles respectively. (Larmin, 1974: 174) These wage figures are all well below adequate income to support a family in comfort. Not surprisingly, Larmin noted that even the most recent wage increases have had no demographic effect.

The inadequate wages of most Soviet workers in urban areas, coupled with rising expectations for improved living standards, are undoubtedly important in the drastic declines in fertility and the high rate of female employment. The wage problem would also explain why so many women continue to work even when they have young children. There is empirical research supporting the relationship between consumption demands and fertility and female employment. A 1966-67 study of family size among Latvian women married since 1959 found that the most important factor in differential fertility was the couple's aspirations for a higher standard of living. (Zvidrin'sh, 1970: 252) A study of urban Ukrainian women found that declining fertility was associated with growing consumption demands and the inability to satisfy them at the present stage of development and production. (Piskunov and Steshenko, 1968: 234-35) Both studies noted that working women had lower fertility than non-working women. Geiger's (1968: 139) book on the Soviet family also reported that desires to improve living standards, to provide opportunities for the children, and for opportunities for women outside the home were the major reasons for Soviet small families.

One consumption problem, that of inadequate housing, has prompted several studies to determine how housing problems affect fertility. A study of over

400 women workers in Moscow, Leningrad, and Penza in 1965-67 found that only about 30% of the women recently married had good housing. The bad housing had resulted in very low birth rates among the women. (Iankova, 1970: 80) Abortion rates as well as low birth rates have been affected by housing conditions, claims Broner (1971). One study Broner refers to showed that in young families, the number of abortions after the first pregnancy was 2 times less in families with more living space than in families with inadequate or low living space. Limiting births after the first child was also closely linked to inadequate living space. (Broner, 1971: 153-54)

Ironically, although inadequate housing is said to promote lower fertility, improving housing has not resulted in increases in fertility, at least after the second child. For example, Merkov (1971: 166) laments that although the housing problem has been virtually solved,[32] the birth rate has not increased nor has the birth of more than two children. The answer to this puzzle is suggested in the findings of Belova and Dar'skii's (1972: 124-25) 1966 and 1969 studies in Moscow. They point out that, although housing is often given as a reason for not having another child, there is often no clear relationship between actual housing conditions (i.e, type of housing or square meters of space per person) and intentions to have another child. Also significant is that in allocating housing, preference is given to families with children.

One could conclude that housing conditions per se do not seem to explain why families have so few children. The explanation appears to be that it is relative and not absolute hardship at work; that is, the standards of acceptable or unacceptable housing are being formed by comparing one's situation to others and to the kind of housing one would like to have (rising consumption standards).

This explanation is supported by Belova and Dar'skii. Although Moscow housing has vastly improved, the number of people who evaluate their housing as unacceptable has increased rather than decreased. The results of 1966 and 1969 studies show that twice as many people in 1969 reported their housing as unsatisfactory as was true in 1966.

Problems of consumption and living standards are also related to the high rate of female employment in urban areas. As mentioned, in families facing severe material hardship, women work largely out of necessity. In more prosperous families the women often work to provide a better standard of living for the family because of career interests or to pursue activities outside the home. Many women also work because they are the head of the household due to widowhood, illegitimacy, or inability to find a husband. (Cf. Mazur, 1973)

c. Cultural "homogenization:" the diffusion of modernization

Although consumption demands have been a major influence on both declining fertility and high female employment, the impact on the Soviet population has been uneven. Until recently, mainly the urban population was affected, and within the urban population social class differences were observed. Since the 1960s, however, modernization, and consequently consumption demands, have been more diffused to other sectors of the population. Alex Inkeles (1968: 143) refers to this diffusion of a more modern urban culture as the "trend toward homogenization." Within urban areas, homogenization can be seen in the greater equalization of wages between manual and service workers. This has important consequences for the spread of consumption values. Inkeles (1968: 143) notes, "The fact that all work for the state leads to uniform and public pay scales, which become a popular standard and shape everyone's expectations, increases the probability of homogenization in earnings. And this, of course, serves in turn to insure relative homogenization in the style of life, in housing, dress, and other consumption patterns."

Housing is one way in which the homogenization of living standards is taking place. Since housing costs are so nominal, workers and highly paid functionaries typically can afford the same housing. (Braverman, 1963: 102) This mixing of the professions and trades better assures a comparison and even imitation of life styles.

Homogenization also has been occurring in the area of family values. This includes similarity of aspirations toward social mobility for oneself and family, similarity in attitudes and tastes, and acceptance of the small-family ideal. (Geiger, 1960: 454; 1968: 188)

Until recently the trend toward cultural homogenization has been largely an urban phenomenon. For one, the cultural and educational levels of the rural areas have, as discussed earlier, long been below those of urban areas. Physical as well as cultural remoteness from modernizing influences has been the rule. Even during the 1950s when living standards were improving, the rural population did not receive nearly the benefits provided the urban popu- lation. Wages lagged far behind those of urban workers. (Cf. Nove, 1969: 337, 365; Bronson and Krueger, 1971: 221-22; Karcz, 1971: 64-65) For example, "In a good Ukrainian kolkhoz, the family receives 30-40 heavy rubles a month from the cooperative and easily doubles this income by direct market sales. But the total monthly income of 100 rubles at most is still less than that of a family of poor workers. In the north of Russia, the income from the coopera- tive may be only one-quarter of this, and sales rarely produce more than 20 rubles a month." (Bronson and Krueger, 1971: 221-22) Moreover, recent income gains have not been accompanied by increases in standard of living. (Karcz, 1971: 64-65) Agricultural work is largely seasonal, performed under adverse conditions, and is far from urban amenities. (Bronson and Krueger, 1971: 237-38) It should also be remembered that it was not until 1965 that collective farmers began to get any state pension.

Despite the disparities that still exist in the level of consumption between the urban and rural populations, conditions are improving in the rural areas. One Soviet report of improving standards of living in the rural areas is provided by Aitov (1969: 134). One encouraging sign of the encroachment of modernization on rural life that Aitov sees is that ". . . a piglet or calf is now rarely seen in a farmer's home." Apparently, such significant changes in the rural life style have been recent.

More important as an indication of changes in the rural areas are the attitudes toward the family and social mobility that are occurring. In the 1960s consumption values and aspirations for a better living standard began making serious inroads. A 1964 study, for instance, showed that rural adults in the region of Sverdlovsk rarely wanted their children to pursue jobs in agriculture. The advice given to many school children from friends and relatives (many of whom had left the rural areas) is to leave the country. (Dodge, 1971: 209)

Rural outmigration reflects the growing aspirations of youth and discontent with rural life. In the earlier years of industrialization and urbanization, a great deal of outmigration was either forced or due to the lack of employment opportunity in the country. Now many rural jobs go begging. Sorlin (1968: 245) accurately states the problem: "The isolated villagers are becoming increasingly aware that they live outside the mainstream of national life.

84

Since distances are enormous, roads bad, and cars few, it is not even possible to take a trip to town on Sundays. The population drift to the cities is due as much to the monotony of rural life as to the uncertainty of agrarian incomes."

Paradoxically, the improvements in education, culture, and living standards that are occurring in the rural areas are promoting outmigration since they raise the level of aspirations and awareness of the gaps between urban and rural life. (Dodge, 1971: 210) But the improvements have done much to change the characteristics of the outmigrant. The rural migrant is now much more like his urban counterpart, in contrast to past migrants who were largely peasant in culture. This has had a significant impact on already low urban birth rates. Volkov (1972: 115-17) observes that recent migrants have values oriented to consumption and requirements of life that are not satisfied in the country. Their family values are also modern. Consequently, rural migrants are now a factor in maintaining the small-family norm associated with the urban population.

Those who remain in the rural areas also are increasingly accepting the small-family idea. (Cf. Geiger, 1968: 188; Peterson, 1969: 540) This is directly related to the diffusion of urban ideas and aspirations for a higher standard of living. This is acknowledged by a leading Soviet demographer, D. Valentei (1974: 307-08), who lists the growth of consumption as the most important factor in declining rural fertility. In fact, Valentei claims that fertility in rural areas only began to decline once production grew and the volume of goods increased; thus consumption and new preferences developed.

The rural population of non-European republics seems to be the only major group still relatively unaffected by modernization and changing consumption preferences. This was shown for example, in Altyeva's (1974) study of rural Turkmen women. Kvasha (1974: 83-84) also provides insights into the conditions of non-European rural areas and the prevalence of consistently high fertility. He notes that manpower rather than mechanization has predominated in agriculture. This encourages the traditional large birth rate. Social mobility is also low due to high agricultural wages. In fact, pay in non-European collective farms is often significantly higher (as much as 40%) than in European collective farms. This disparity in income could conceivably be a major factor in not only non-European immobility, but European migration from rural areas to cities where prospects are brighter.

Family Policy: An Evaluation

So far in this chapter, I have discussed how modernization, especially through the growth of consumption and living standards, has affected the fertility and female labor force trends in the Soviet Union. This was done in order to better understand the role of family policy, whose goals were to promote both high fertility and female employment. I have tried to show that fertility declined as new consumer preferences developed and aspirations for a better standard of living spread in urban areas and later to the countryside. Female employment has grown steadily, but in urban areas, the main factors have been the material hardships of urban areas or higher standards of what comprises an acceptable style of life. In rural areas, female employment is traditional and in many cases seasonal rather than full time. It is little related to modernization or declining fertility as is true of urban areas.

The question at this point is how family policies affected fertility and female employment given the fact that level of modernization seems to be the major force at work in both differential fertility and employment. I would conclude that, especially since 1960, family policies have, on the whole, had little lasting impact. In the late 1940s and 1950s there was some cause for optimism. Both fertility and female labor force participation were increasing. And, undoubtedly, the benefits and services offered to mothers and families with children were helpful in offsetting some of the hardships of the postwar years. As late as 1963, one of the USSR's foremost demographers, B. Urlanis (1963: 30-31), maintained that the family laws and benefits they provided "represented a great landmark in Soviet population policy." Fertility increased significantly in following years and, Urlanis claimed, government policies had a great deal to do with it.

By the 1960s, however, as fertility rates began to decline sharply, it became increasingly evident to Soviet and Western observers alike that the policies were ineffective. As was discussed earlier, the government was compelled to liberalize the divorce procedure due to the high rate of divorce and illegitimate unions resulting from restrictive policies. By the 1970s, one of three Soviet marriages reportedly ends in divorce within 3 years or less; and the official rates do not include unregistered divorces--30% in Moscow alone. (Cohn, 1973: 52-53) Also in the 1960s, support for illegitimate children was curtailed. Such incentive measures as child care facilities and maternity benefits have proved to be inadequate to the need despite improvements that have occurred. Moreover, such benefits do not significantly defray the costs of children. In the cities, according to Kvasha (1974: 150-54), the costs of rearing a child, including the mother's loss of income when she can't work because a child is ill, are higher than most families can manage. And with the constant growth in standards, the costs of raising a child are increasing.

At best, the child care facilities available have kept fertility from falling even lower than it has, especially among working women in urban areas. This conclusion is reached by H. Cohn (1973: 51) in her recent investigation of Soviet population policy. Cohn remarks that if massive day care construction had not been undertaken in the 1960s, the birth rate decline may have been greater.

Similar conclusions can be made about family allowances. Monetary aids may well have helped in some cases to prevent a more drastic decline in fertility. However, as allowances were cut and became an increasingly small proportion of the family's income, their incentive value declined. Furthermore, it could be argued that most of the women having large families would have done so anyway because of cultural traditions or economic conditions favoring large families. Perhaps payments could encourage these women to have even larger families than usual, but this is speculative. A major reason for the ineffectiveness of family allowances, however, is that most Soviet families are not even eligible for payments. In 1960, for example, only about 20% of Soviet families were eligible for any payments. (Heer and Bryden, 1966: 156-57)

Soviet experts have also begun to take note of the inadequacy of family allowances as stimulants to childbearing. A. Kvasha (1968: 73-74) concludes that the number of children in low fertility regions has not been raised as a result of family allowances. Women who must work or who desire to work find additional children a tremendous burden. Payments do not compensate for these problems. Perhaps the best comment on the inadequacy of allowances is offered by Zvidrin'sh (1970: 256): "The article position on government aid to parents has little effect in the conditions of the Latvian SSR, but also in

88

some other union republics. Monthly payments begin with the birth of the fourth child. While for the overwhelming majority of families of the republic the usual problem is the question of the birth even of a second child."

Abortion policy has also been unsuccessful. Forbidding abortions in 1944 resulted mainly in an increase in illegal abortions; therefore, it was relegalized in 1955. Forbidding abortion, if it affected anything, contributed to a decline in female employment, since women forced to conceive might have to quit work or be unable to work. More importantly, legalizing abortion undoubtedly has contributed to the declining fertility of Soviet women; since, abortion, legal or illegal, is the main method of birth control used. Interestingly, the birth rate did not decline after abortion was relegalized in 1955 despite the fact that registered abortions tripled. (Sadvokasova, 1968: 220; Ovcharov, 1966: 55) This suggests that in the 1950s legalized abortion made little difference in the actual frequency of abortion. However, after 1960, as the need and desire for family limitation spread, abortion became more prevalent. It cannot be said, though, that abortion was a cause of lower fertility; abortion was only a means. At any rate, abortion is widely practiced, and repeated abortions are common. In a 1970 study of abortion among women 35-39 in Moscow, 54% had 1-3 abortions. Almost 25% had between 4-10 abortions. Only 22% of women had never had an abortion. (Larmin, 1974: 87) David Heer (1965: 535-36) concluded that abortions may well equal the number of live births and that the frequency of abortion in the USSR may be as high as anywhere in the world. Mehlan (1966: 213-14) supports Heer by his report that in large cities and industrial districts abortions equal live births. The frequency of abortion is much lower, however, in rural districts and non-European populations.

Most Soviet experts conclude that forbidding abortion is an ineffective way to increase fertility. It is argued that forbidding abortion would only lead to harmful consequences such as higher mortality from criminal abortion, an increase in sterility among women, and the birth of unwanted children who could not be properly brought up. (Kiseleva, 1968: 155; Sadvokasova, 1968: 224; Merkov, 1971: 165-66) More frequently, contraceptives are being encouraged as an alternative to abortion. At the same time, the family's conscious control of births is accepted by the government as a reality with which it must live. Other methods to increase the birth rate are being emphasized (see chapter 4), although success to date is questionable.

On the whole, an evaluation of Soviet family policy would be that it has been an ineffective set of measures for increasing fertility and, at the same time, ensuring a high rate of female employment. While it is true that a large proportion of women work, Soviet family policy has had relatively little to do with this. Moreover, high female employment has been coupled with low levels of fertility. The reason fertility has declined and female employment has increased is largely a result of modernization and social change. This conclusion is drawn also by Inkeles and Bauer (1968: 193) in their study, The Soviet Citizen:

> Our data strongly suggest that most Soviet families were relatively unaffected in any direct way by the swing of Soviet family legislation. At least insofar as the law was concerned, marriage and family life went on pretty much as before.

The family did, however, undergo many changes as a product of the developments in Soviet society.

> These effects were not, however, the direct result of official family policy but rather the indirect result of the broader

processes of social change which the regime set in motion. . . .
The greatest of these forces are industrialization and the collectivization of agriculture.

In the next chapter, the influence of Soviet ideology on family policy
will be examined. Although practical economic and social realities, as discussed, were a major factor in the formulation and changes of family policies,
the Soviet perception (or misperception, I should say) of these realities
was colored by Marxist-Leninist theory. The Soviet ideological view influenced the direction of family policies (since ideology often stipulated
the problem). However, as will be seen, the Soviets have not been immune to
the realities of fertility and female employment trends since the 1960s.
The Soviets have also become aware of the failures of their family policies
to date. The result is that ideology has been undergoing a transformation
which may well signal the direction of family policies in the future.

CHAPTER 4

SOVIET MARXISM AND FAMILY POLICY

An analysis of Soviet family policy would be incomplete unless the role of Soviet Marxism is taken into account; since the principles of Soviet Marxism, as outlined by Marx, Engels, and Lenin serve as the theoretical basis of Soviet policy. In their efforts to create a new society, the Soviets stress that theory and practice must correspond. This justifies the use of policy to achieve theoretically stipulated ends. So far, I have emphasized how family policy in the Soviet Union was influenced by the exigencies of the postwar period. But, as briefly discussed in chapter 1, theoretical conceptions of demographic phenomena, particularly reproduction, also played an important role in the formulation of family policy and its objectives. But to understand how family policy and ideology are related presupposes some understanding of Marxism.

Essential in Soviet ideology is the Marxist conception of dialectical materialism, historical stages and laws, and human action in history. These theoretical elements also prevade Soviet population theory. In the following discussion, Soviet ideology and its bearing on Soviet family policy will be examined. It will be seen that Soviet ideology and its bearing on Soviet family policy will be examined. It will be seen that Soviet ideology until the early 1960s was strongly pronatalist, as was family policy. After the

1960s when fertility declined rapidly, the earlier conceptions of both theory and policy came under increasing attack. The result has been reappraisal and modification of both the ideology of population and family policy.

Soviet Marxist Theory

The basic underlying principle of Marxism is the dialectic. According to this view, everything is in a process of change and development. Change is viewed as an inherent quality of all matter (i.e., natural or social phenomena subject to scientific investigation) due to internal "contradictions." Contradications are due to the working of opposing forces that produce conflict. For example, in human history all societies are in a process of change and movement toward new, and higher, forms of development or stages; e.g., the feudal stage was succeeded by capitalism which, in turn, gives way to the higher stages of socialism and finally communism. In each stage, contradictions, based on the conflicts of opposing economic classes (those who own and those who do not own the means of production), are fundamentally responsible for change. Although change is posited as an inherent quality, it does not occur randomly, but on the basis of objectively discernible "laws" unique to each historical stage. Since each historical stage is characterized by and develops in accordance with its own laws, Marxists believe that man can effect his own history if he can correctly determine the laws of development. (Cf. Wetter, 1958: 312, 317-18, 334-35)

Most Marxists understand "law" differently than it is often conceived. For one, a law is not a timeless generalization applying to all times and places. Laws are historically limited. They could be considered as patterns of interaction or social structures that are qualitatively different in different historical stages. Another difference, often a source of confusion even among Marxists, is that laws are not necessary or inevitable events like physical laws that are external to human activity. (Venable, 1945: 171-213) When Marx spoke of the "inevitable" collapse of capitalism, for instance, he was referring to the fact that cumulative weakening trends inherent in capitalism would, if continued, eventually lead to a point where the system could no longer support itself. But this all involved human action and decision-making. "The defeat . . . is inevitable not apart from what any people do, but precisely because of what people do because they are people." (Somerville, 1967: 100-01) Rather than being pawns on the historical stage, men can control historical change as they correctly understand the processes at work and consciously create the social and economic conditions necessary for the old system to fail and the new to emerge. (Somerville, 1967: 99)

In the USSR the role of men in historical change is strongly emphasized. It is embodied in the belief that the Party is the agent responsible for the correct formulation and actualizing of the "laws of socialism;" that is, the pattern of institutions and relationships that characterize socialism, the stage in which the transition to the classless society occurs. Soviet writings stress action--the building of communism--not inevitability.

Although Marxists believe that objective laws exist, the formulation of these laws may be only partially correct (since our knowledge never exhausts reality, we only approximate truth through our reflections of it in our theories). Yet, as mentioned above, Marxists claim that men control history by a correct understanding of the objective laws of history. The solution to this seeming contradiction is the notion of a dialectic between theory and action. The Soviets refer to this as the "unity of theory and action."

94

Theory is considered the basis of action, but (successful) action is the criterion of truth for theory. (Wetter, 1958: 263-64)

The brief discussion above of Soviet Marxist principles explains much of the Soviet belief in planning and the use of comprehensive policies to bring social reality in line with theory. Moreover, the doctrines of the unity of theory and action and the partial nature of knowledge allows for the correction and reinterpretation of theory in light of experience. It is important to keep in mind that generally the Soviets sincerely view their policies as instrumental in bringing about the transition from socialism to communism. This requires that the vestiges of capitalist relations are erased and that the implementation of the laws of socialism (which the Soviets admit are still imperfectly understood) is accomplished. At such a time, the classless communist society will be a reality.

The insistence on the correspondence of policy with theory and purported laws of socialism may seem idiosyncratic, if not a severe stricture in dealing with social problems. Indeed, Soviet history supplies well-known instances that support this; e.g., the efforts in the 1920s to render the family obsolete despite popular opposition. There are benefits, however, to the Soviet position. One is that the Soviets avoid the ad hoc approach of dealing with problems which is sometimes characteristic of more democratic societies having no comprehensive societal program or view of the future. Another benefit is that the Soviets are able to evaluate the efficacy of policy in light of explicit theoretical expectations and to make changes accordingly.

95

The Laws of Population: The Roots of Soviet Pronatalism

Among the laws characterizing any historical stage are laws of population. Laws of population were first expounded by Marx and Engels in Capital. In capitalism, Marx and Engels claimed, the law of population involves unemployment and poverty due to the process of accumulation. This resulted in "relative overpopulation" of the working class who comprised a "surplus army." Marx's position was in sharp opposition to Malthus, considered a bourgeois apologist. Malthus proposed that absolute overpopulation occurs due to the tendency of population to exceed the level of subsistence. Marxists, by contrast, blamed capitalist exploitation and inequities in distribution for population problems. Malthus was also attacked because he was proposing a universal law of population for human societies. Marx insisted that each socio-economic formation has its own laws. (Cf. Valentei, 1971: 437)

Being historically based, the law of population under capitalism would not apply beyond capitalism itself. In socialism a new law of population comes into existence. The ownership of the means of production is no longer in the hands of profit-seeking individuals, but in the hands of society as a whole. Therefore, production would serve societal needs, not the interests of a few capitalists. In opposition to capitalism, full employment, planned and proportionate development, and rational use of productive resources become subsumed under the socialist law of population. In socialism new technology would not result in unemployment, poverty, or a surplus army but in a shortening of the work day and a release from toil. (Guzevatyi, 1970: 37) Consequently, overpopulation would not be a problem, nor population growth a source of concern. Instead, socialism would promote high growth rates and reproduction.

Until the mid-1960s, the Soviets interpreted the law of population in socialism as a mandate for rapid population growth and high birth rates. In 1940, for instance, Sul'kevich (1940: 8-10), who was head of the census bureau, wrote that Engels himself regarded high reproductive levels as evidence of the prosperity of the workers. After the 1939 census, Sul'kevich proudly noted that population growth and reproduction levels were higher than in capitalist Europe. This was proof that scientific communism was correct and that capitalism was an obstacle to population growth. "So the rapid growth of population of the national republics and regions testifies to the growth of prosperity of the people of the USSR and most of all to the victory of Leninist-Stalinist national policy."

The linking of rapid population growth and prosperity is also attributed to Lenin's theory of imperialism. Lenin proposed that declining fertility in capitalist countries was a sign of the growing "crisis of capitalism." As the contradictions of capitalism became more intense and the worker's condition became more miserable, workers had to lower their family size in order to survive. Once the source of contradictions and human misery are removed--namely capitalism itself--population would grow. The Soviets interpreted this to mean that any slowing or cessation of population growth was a sign of decay. (Dallin, 1947: 131-32)

It is not surprising that from 1944 until very recently Soviet ideology has been translated into pronatalist policies. On both the domestic and foreign policy levels, the Soviets have been consistently pronatalist, and falling birth rates have been viewed with alarm.

In foreign policy until recently,[33] the Soviets have manifested their pronatalist ideology in a virulent opposition to family planning programs in underdeveloped nations. High birth rates were considered desirable for the continued struggle against capitalism. The Soviets viewed the poor of the underdeveloped world as members of the proletariat and part of the common struggle against capitalist exploitation. Their hunger, poverty, and unemployment were due solely to colonial and neocolonial oppression not to overpopulation or high birth rates. In one book on population by Pisarev (1962: 52-53), Western alarm over population growth is rejected. Referring to Lenin's work on the working class and Neo-Malthusianism, Pisarev discredits concern over population growth because the working class is being told that the cause of their situation is the birth rate, rather than capitalism. Pisarev answers that the working class rejects this--they are not doomed to perish but to grow and become more strong.

Soviet opposition to lowering the birth rate and family planning programs was expressed in numerous publications in the 1950s with such lurid titles as the following:

> "Present Malthusianism--Manhating Ideology of Imperialism"
> "American Imperialists' Ideology is Cannibals' Ideology"
> "Expose the Warmongers' Ideology"
> "Fanatical Delirium of Contemporary Malthusians"
> (Petersen, 1964: 113-17)

I have already discussed Soviet pronatalism in domestic policy. High birth rates were desired and government policy was used to insure this. In the 1950s S. Strumilin (1968: 19) reflected the Soviet position:

> . . . in conditions of competition with capitalism, every
> worker is on record and a high birth rate is deliberately
> encouraged by the Party and the Government. Here mass birth
> control--a practice obviously detrimental to both the health
> instincts of motherhood and the interests of the country--

though not prohibited is hardly deserving of public approval.

And in 1957 publication, Strumilin (in Brackett, 1968: 162) made it clear that declining fertility would be met by policies to counter such a trend even to the point of eliminating contraceptives and abortion. Notably, Strumilin's remarks were made two years after the relegalization of abortion and may have been a threat intended to discourage its overuse.

The Soviets continued into the early 1960s to try to work out the law of population in socialism on the basis of a pronatalist interpretation. For example, Pisarev in his book, Population of the USSR, discusses the issues of population laws and population dynamics. Although he talks a great deal about the law of population for socialism, he remarks that there really is no consensus as to the actual content of the law. There is one consensus noted-- the law for socialism is the opposite of the capitalist law of population! Pisarev adds that the socialist law of population is the foundation of demographic regularities in socialist countries. This law allows for the continual growth of prosperity for the workers and, consequently, the lowering of morbidity and mortality along with a preservation of a high level of fertility. (Pisarev, 1962: 34)

As a contrast to socialism, Pisarev (1962: 18-34) provides an analysis of population trends in the West. He claims that declining fertility is due to declining living standards and exploitation, not to increasing prosperity. This is in direct opposition to the theory of the demographic transition, by which Western demographers account for fertility decline as a result of ris- ing living standards and increasing prosperity. Pisarev also ignores that in most cases an inverse relationship between fertility and prosperity is usually found in demographic research.

The 1960s: Pronatalism Weakened

The view that fertility declined because of poor living conditions and capitalist productive relations began to come under challenge at about the time Pisarev wrote his book. This challenge was inevitable because, as Soviet demographic statistics were showing, the USSR itself was undergoing the steady decline in fertility levels that were discussed in chapter 3. The Soviets could no longer contend that declining birth rates were a sign of decay or crisis when their own birth rates were falling! In 1963, a leading Soviet demographer, B. Urlanis (1963: 64-69), wrote a book on Soviet trends in which he noted that such factors as higher cultural levels, women in the work force, and rising consumption standards were producing a decline in the birth rate.

Further weakening of the pronatalist conception of the socialist law of population occurred in the late 1960s as the contradiction of theory with Soviet reality became increasingly apparent. In 1966 D. Broner (1966: 66) pointed out that the supposed rapid growth of population expected in socialism was not verified by the statistics. B. Boldyrev (1968: 75-80) added that fertility was also steadily declining, not only in the USSR, but in other socialist countries as well. Moreover, if the rapid growth considered theoretically ideal became a universal reality, the world would be over-populated in 3-4 centuries. Boldyrev's remark was in marked disagreement with Soviet orthodoxy, in which only relative overpopulation was considered possible. In another attack on orthodoxy, A. Volkov (1968: 171) called "dognatic," hence incorrect, the longheld position that a lowering of fertility was character-istic only of capitalism.

The relationship between reproduction and prosperity began to undergo considerable revision. As mentioned, Urlanis' book noted that fertility

declines were linked to rising cultural and material standards. But it was

Guzevatyi (1968: 10-12; 1970: 32-33) who soundly refuted the pronatalist

position by pointing to the contradictions in Soviet society. In socialism,

he noted, the level of fertility was supposed to increase. It has, however,

been declining. The reasons are economic and cultural progress, education,

participation of women in the work force, and higher demands for a good

standard of living. Those who think high fertility areas are evidence of the

socialist law of population are wrong. These areas are the least progressive

in the USSR. The most consumption and higher living standards in differential

fertility is now generally recognized by Soviet demographers. (Cf. Smulevich,

1970; Valentei, 1971, 1974; Aper'ian, 1971; Vzhilianskii, 1973; Sonin, 1974)

The Soviets were also compelled to deal with the fact that, rather

than differeing from the West, Soviet demographic trends closely resemble

those of Western countries. All have low mortality and low or moderate

fertility with low or moderate growth rates. Boldyrev (1968: 93-94) was an

early revisionist of the Soviet position that high fertility and growth were

the characteristic pattern in socialism. Instead, he asserted that the effect

of socialism on reproduction was to create the possibility for the "rapid

turn to a more progressive type of reproduction of population." By "progres-

sive" he meant the pattern of fertility and mortality characteristic of

developed capitalist countries. Boldyrev was quick to distinguish, however,

that socialism still differs from capitalism. Socialism brings the tran-

sition to low fertility about much more quickly than capitalism. Boldyrev's

discussion is a significant change in Soviet ideology.

The theoretical problem created by the similarity in demographic rates between the West and the USSR has been handled by the theorists in a typically Marxist way. The Soviets insist that each socio-economic formation has its own laws, and they deny that demographic phenomena in capitalism and socialism can be encompassed in the same theory (there are no universal laws). For example, in some recent works, notably Valentei's (1974) book on Marxist-Leninist population theory, references are made to demographic stages and the demographic transition. However, the relevance of the theory of the demographic rates is denied by Soviet theorists. It is not acceptable to explain the similarity in demographic rates (the quantitative) between the USA and the USSR in terms of such generalities as the "form of life of industrial society." These similarities hide the deep socio-economic differences in each society (the qualitative) that provide the true basis for adequate explanation. (Valentei, 1971: 452-53; Kvasha, 1974: 58)

In most cases, fertility decline in capitalist countries is still explained in negative terms--mainly that the demands of present production for labor compels parents to provide education and professional training for their children so that they can compete in the "struggle for work." In other words, hardship and economic insecurity (e.g., fear of recession and unemployment due to the business cycle) are behind the change to small families. In socialism, however, lower fertility is positive and progressive because it reflects the general spread of higher cultural and material aspirations and attainments.

Reinterpreting the Laws of Population

As we have seen, the need for radical changes in the Soviet interpretation of the laws of population, especially the law for socialism, was

102

brought about by the changes in fertility occurring in the USSR. The general decline in fertility plus the Soviets' own demographic data suggested that the decline would continue and that growing prosperity and consumption standards were the chief reasons. Rather than discarding the law of population in socialism, the Soviets have been putting energy into reinterpreting the law and making it more consistent with actual trends.

One of the first changes concerned what was meant by a "law" of population. Pisarev (1962: 708) had considered a law to be a concrete, necessary connection between phenomena. On the other hand, there are "regularities" which are processes causally determined by a whole combination of laws. The laws of population, according to Pisarev, are economic, not demographic laws that apply only to the working class. But the laws are manifested in demographic regularities; e.g., in socialism there is high fertility. The idea that population laws are necessary or inevitable has now been discarded. Smulevich (1970: 23) and Valentei (1974: 15-17) viewed it as a "mistake" to have regarded laws as inevitable. Rather, laws are tendencies which are realized in the concrete struggle with countertendencies, hardships, and contradictions. This theme is expressed by Smulevich (1970: 20) when he criticizes those who believed that the socialist law of population would come into effect automatically and without contradiction. Problems still exist in socialism. Smulevich's position here is an emphasis on the active role of men in bringing about the conditions for the laws to work. This position also provides a graceful excuse for the fact that fertility is not as high as expected; there are still contradictions to be worked out first.

Another change in ideology involved the nature of the relationship of laws of population and demographic phenomena. (See Larmin, 1972 and

Vzhilianskii, 1973, who discuss the evolution of the Soviet debate on this issue.) The earliest position (into the 1950s) was that demographic trends were the direct products of the economic structure. With men such as Pisarev (early 1960s), the distinction is made that the laws of population are economic not demographic; yet demograhpic regularities are still assumed to be determined by and to differ depending on the economic structure. By the late 1960s, further distinctions are made between the laws of population and demographics. Dzarasova (1968: 45-46) maintains that laws of population, as developed by Marx, apply only to the employment of the population. Marx was not concerned with population per se. Reproduction of the entire population requires its own set of laws based on actual concrete study of the situation. Guzevatyi (1970: 30-31, 36-37) agrees and adds that the eclectic combining of economic and demographic phenomena is fruitless and should be avoided.

A related problem concerns efforts to formulate demographic laws. The Soviets at this point have resolved the question by emphasizing the role superstructural factors play in population dynamics at the expense of the economic base. Guzevatyi (1968: 14) remarks, "Although fertility, mortality, and other demographic phenomena depend on the economic system of the society, this dependence is mediated by a number of factors of the superstructural level such as national tradition and custom, legal institutions, and social aims." In a later work he even charges the official Bol'shaia Sovetskaia Entsiklopedia with "oversimplification" and "absolutization" of socio-economic factors in its characterization of the socialist law of population. (Guzevatyi, 1970: 30-31) Another expert concludes that it is especially difficult to establish a direct relationship between fertility and the means of production due to ethnic, national, socio-cultural, and social psychological factors.

104

(Kozlov, 1969: 106)

The result of the reinterpretation of the law of population is that
now there is only minor correspondence between the law of population (an
economic law) and demographic phenomena. The former is the province of
economics, the latter are a subject for demography and other social sciences.
It is of great significance that demographic phenomena are given considerable
autonomy from the economic base, while in earlier conceptions, they were
wholly dependent on it. This is shown by the change in the definition of the
socialist law of population in some publications. Whereas Smulevich (1970:
25-26) characterized the law as the rational use of labor resources and the
rational reproduction of population, Valentei (1974: 21) does not include
population reproduction as part of his definition. Rather Valentei (1974:
21-22) stresses that demographic regularities depend on the "totality of
social relations," not just productive relations.

The recognition of the dependence of demographic events on many factors,
rather than simply on a socialist economic base, was a necessary change in
ideology. In the USSR the case has been that demographic trends have not been
very amenable to either the change to a socialist economy or to narrowly
conceived family policies that did not take into account the "totality" of
social relations. The changes in Soviet ideology are creating the basis for
a more flexible approach to family policy and a greater recognition of the
variety of factors that influence fertility.

Theory and Family Policy Since 1960

The effort to correctly formulate the law of population for socialism
remains a major concern of Soviet demographers despite disagreement as to its

actual content. There is at least general agreement that the socio-economic

formation is connected with and affects demographic phenomena (along with

other factors) and that socialism, being the highest stage of development

achieved, creates the most "progressive" demographic conditions such as low

mortality and increased longevity. The question of "progressive" fertility

has not been solved, however. It is true that high fertility levels and the

large family ideal have been rejected. As E. Rosset (1974: 62) puts it, the

large family is a thing of the past. "Today the struggle is not for the

fourth or fifth child, but for the second and third child." In place of high

fertility norms, the ambiguous concept "optimal fertility" is increasingly

prevalent in the literature; i.e., fertility should not be high or low but at

a level harmonious with both family and societal needs. (Cf. Kvasha, 1974:

93-133; Valentei, 1974: 20-69) In the present context of Soviet society,

optimal fertility means that where fertility is too low (the European, mainly

urban population) it should be raised; and where it is too high (mainly the

non-European, rural population), it should be lowered.

Theoretical concern about optimal fertility has its parallel in policy

concerns. In 1968 at the All-Union Symposium on Regional Fertility serious

attention was directed toward the problems of differential fertility.

(Kiseleva, 1968) The alarm over high fertility seems to be due largely to

fears that non-European minorities will become a larger proportion of the

population (reminiscent of tsarist Slavophilism). And indeed, the 1970 census

shows that Europeans are becoming a smaller percent of the population compared

to 1959 while non-European groups have increased. (TsSU, Vol. 4, 1973: 9)

Soviet writers also fear the problems created by large non-European families.

Kvasha (1974: 70-83) writes that large families are detrimental to the "quality"

106

of the population. Large families are traditional; and in large families, children are not provided the care and benefits smaller families offer.

Although high fertility is now considered a problem rather than an asset in Soviet society, low fertility is still the major concern. Many demographers fear that the population will no longer reproduce itself if families continue to have only one or two children. (Cf. Rosset, 1974: 64-65) Aging of the population is also frequently mentioned as an economic and social problem. But, without a doubt, the inability to meet labor force needs is the most serious threat posed by continued low fertility. (More will be said about this below.)

In response to theoretical changes and practical problems involving fertility, criticisms and reevaluations of past policies are frequent. Reporting on the All-Union Symposium on the Theory of Population, Kozyrev (1967: 142) frankly admits the failure of both theory and policy in the area of fertility. Fertility trends have not been amenable to much control. Guzevetyi (1968: 20-21) called the efforts of government policy to promote uniformly high fertility a "mistaken view." And Kiseleva (1968: 154-55) glumly reported that in republics with high or low fertility, there is no evidence that the rates are going to change in direction; and a population policy to deal with these "harmful trends" is needed.

The ensuring debate over policies to bring fertility to an optimal level has shown the Soviets to be aware of the main causes of the problem and also of the flaws in past policies especially those aimed at encouraging the birth rate. Rather than a uniform policy for all groups, stress is laid on the need for what Kvasha (1974: 83) calls "a variegated complex of measures geared to all layers of society and groups." This means taking into account such differences as tradition, consumption desires, and income and education.

Where fertility is too low, the necessity of coping with the problem of consumption is generally considered the only hope for a significant increase in the birth rate. The gap between material and cultural demand and the capacity of Soviet production to meet the demand is recognized as a major cause of low fertility. Policies have failed in the past largely because the problems of consumption and the "family's interests" were not adequately dealt with. Raising consumption is considered so important by Aper'ian (1971: 149) that he believes a policy to counteract declining fertility is not likely to be effective at the present stage of economic and social development. On the same note, Vzhilianskii (1973: 69) concludes that only an economic policy offers a lasting impact on the birth rate. Any purely demographic policy, such as forbidding abortion or contraceptive devices, will not have a profound or lasting effect no matter how actively it is pursued. Even Marx's theory of population, claims Vzhilianskii, stressed that demographic as well as social development depends on progress in social production. The present intensification of production naturally leads to lower fertility. As this process produces greater labor productivity and a higher standard of living, fertility will increase.

In dealing with the problem of consumption and fertility, most Soviet writers have believed that increasing goods and services, or else building communisum (when production can fully satisfy consumption demands), will bring about an increase in fertility. There are suggestions, however, that this is not the case. M. Sonin (1974: 98-99) has developed an intriguing theoretical model dealing with the relationship between fertility and

consumption. He calls his work the model of the "hierarchy of needs."
Sonin's model is important in several ways. For one, Sonin draws conclusions
at variance with those who believe that meeting current consumption demands
will increase fertility. Also Sonin's model has some novel implications for
family policy that are worth discussing in some detail.

Sonin bases his model on Marx and Lenin's "law of increasing needs,"
which describes the relationship between consumption and fertility. Adapted
to the USSR, Sonin distinguishes four stages in Soviet history: the 1930s,
the 1970s, socialism, and communism. Also listed are five consumption "needs"
which assume different priority in each stage: needs for work, living
conditions, children, free time, and education. The need for children is of
special interest here. In the 1970s Sonin places children at the bottom of
the list! This undoubtedly reflects the already discussed relationship
between consumption and low fertility since the 1960s. It also suggests that
Sonin expects no change during the decade of the 1970s. However, in socialism
(no specific date given), which is being developed, children move to second
place in importance due to "social responsibility." Since the socialist
stage is the one in which the basis of communism is laid, the implication is
that families must be convinced that it is their duty to have more children
in order to achieve communism. Once communism is achieved, the fourth stage,
the importance of children changes considerably. Children become next to last
in importance! Sonin explains that once communism is built, the economy is
labor intensive and population growth will "lose its significance."

Sonin's position is a significant change from the view that in socialism
and communism the basis for population growth is laid, or that meeting consumption demands will bring about higher fertility. On the contrary, Sonin

is saying that meeting consumption demands brings about new demands through the "law of increasing needs." Children decline further in priority.
Another implication of Sonin's model is that a policy to promote fertility must be one in which the family's social responsibility is emphasized. This is similar to the Soviet expression of a "harmony between the family's and society's interests." A further inference could be drawn. The family's interests in a small number of children (only 1 or 2), since consumption of the fruits of modernization are a greater priority, are contrary to society's need for more children. Thus, left to itself without government interference, there would seem to be no reason for the family to have more children. In fact, as modernization spreads to rural and non-European areas, fertility should decline further if Sonin is correct.

It cannot be determined how influential Sonin's work is on either population theory or policy. It may be that the Soviets would draw different conclusions about the model's implications that I have. At least one demographer, however, has pointed out that efforts to support the birth of two and three children must cope with the widespread problem of "veshchism," the fetish with "things." Communism rejects the mindless pursuit of the material (beyond basic needs); the spiritual (including raising children) is to be promoted instead. (Larmin, 1974: 191-92) At any rate, most Soviet demographers propose measures that optimistically relate fertility increases to economic improvements and government aid to families.

The types of measures currently being proposed to deal with the fertility problem are of three main types: (1) economic, (2) administrative-judicial, and (3) propagandistic-moral. A combination of all three types is usually advocated but differences exist. Many suggestions involve changes or expansion of old policies.

In the late 1960s experts such as Mehlan (1966: 215), Broner (1968: 80) and Guzevatyi (1968: 12) stressed economic measures, such as providing childcare facilities, housing, benefits to mothers, and domestic services as the way to increase fertility. They believed that meeting consumption demands at the level then current would result in higher fertility. In addition to these specific measures, Valentei (1969: 57) suggested that equalization of living standards (i.e., amenities of life and real wages) in all regions of the country would stimulate the birth rate. Essentially, this proposal amounts to advocating the continued expansion of the Soviet economy.

Increasing benefits to mothers, especially those who work, has been widely promoted. Increases in the postnatal leave time, shorter work days for mothers of young children, more leave time without pay for mothers, and possibilities for mothers to work at home are mentioned. (Valentei, 1969: 58-59) Another suggestion is to pay women 30-50% of their wage (up to 100-120 rubles per month) to stay home with new babies up to one year old. (Larmin, 1974: 183-184) One benefit program, family allowances, has come under increasing attack. Valentei (1969: 58-59) advocates the abolition of family allowances as well as benefits for mothers of illegitimate children. These benefits do not improve the well-being of recipients and are a "squandering" of government funds. After examining the allowance programs of the USSR and other countries, Vzhilianskii (1973: 54-55) similarly concludes that allowances do not result in any significant and stable rise in the birth rate. Moreover, the payments may well lower needed female employment and unskilled household labor.

Rather than abolishing family allowances, Kvasha (1968: 77; 1974: 160-61) recommends changes in the program. As presently constituted, no monthly payments are given until after the birth of the fourth child, and the amount is very low. If allowances are to encourage fertility in areas where only one and two children are being born, then substantial payments must begin with the first birth and increase thereafter. Three-child families should have most expenses paid since material reasons are the major hindrance to childbearing. The payments should continue until the child is 16. To prevent a lowering of family income, temporarily nonworking mothers of small children should be compensated for loss of pay.

Other family policy proposals involve administrative-judicial and propagandistic-moral policies. Kvasha (1974: 146-50) discusses these proposals at some length. He suggests, for one, the possibility of prohibiting the production and sale of birth control devices and forbidding abortion. (He is the only one I have read who mentions this in recent years.) Lowering or raising the minimum marriage age and providing privileges to families with children are other suggestions; e.g., exemption from military duty for fathers of large families, income tax benefits, lower housing and service costs. Propaganda could be used to disseminate information on the dangers of abortion, the happiness and honor of motherhood or fatherhood, and the necessity of having two or three children.

Kvasha is not trying to promote large families, however. In fact, he believes large families are negative in terms of the development and professional education of mothers, and through them, of the children. Mother heroines (10 children or more) are pointed to by Kvasha as a salient example of the bad consequences of large families. (This is particularly striking

112

since Mother Heroine is the nation's highest award to mothers.) Most mother heroines do not work and almost none are service workers or more scientific workers. On the whole, they are housewives and kolkhoz and sovkhoz (farm) workers. (Kvasha, 1974: 83)

Significantly, one family policy that appears to have declined in prominence is state takeover of the family's childrearing functions through communal institutions. Early in the Soviet period, the state's assumption of childrearing and other domestic functions was a much heralded goal. Even in the 1960s much attention was paid to the construction of boarding schools and schools of the prolonged day as a way for the state to lessen the family's "burdens" by keeping children away most of the time. (Cf. Dodge, 1966; Bronfenbrenner, 1968)

Hopefully, state takeover of major family responsibilities in child-rearing would also encourage the birth rate; since most of the reasons for a small family (i.e., the costs of childrearing) would be removed. The reason for rejecting state takeover is largely economic. Kvasha (1974: 138) figures that in 1970 there were 70 million children up to age 14 in the USSR. To provide one place in a child care center costs the government almost 890 rubles. Obviously, the cost of child care for all would be astronomical. Other problems with state takeover are that traditional family values are in opposition to such a policy and that psychological and social problems for both child and parents can result.

The Soviet Dilemma: Fertility or Female Employment

It was mentioned earlier that the main reason for Soviet concern over low fertility is their labor force demands. More needs to be said about this.

The Soviets describe optimal fertility as that which corresponds to society's interests, not just the family's. By society's interests is meant the building of communism. The building of communism is in many ways a matter of transforming the productive base of society and, as Valentei (1974: 20-69) discusses, labor is the main productive force. Only through economic development and the expansion of production can the elimination of class differences, unemployment, and the gaps between city and country or mental and physical work be achieved. And these are the central goals of Marxism-Leninism.

Low fertility is seen as such a serious threat to economic development because a large and expanding labor force is essential to Soviet production. As Sonin (1974: 99) recognizes, the socialist stage is labor extensive and population growth is essential. The problem is that growth in the Soviet labor force has been declining since the 1960s due to declining population growth since the 1940s. From 1960-65 the average yearly increase in the number of workers, service workers, and collective farmers was 11.5 million. From 1965-70 the increase declined to 11.4 million. The estimate for 1970-75 showed only 10 million new workers. The percentage of working-age population has also been contracting. In 1959 about 58% of the population was of working age; in 1970--54%. (Vzhilianskii, 1973: 52)

It is the European republics that have shown the least increase in working-age population since 1959. In the USSR as a whole the working-age population has increased in numbers by 9% (although it is a smaller proportion of the population). The rate of increase in European republics range from 5-19%; non-European republics have grown by 18-31%. Although migration of young people from European to non-European republics is to some degree involved in these age figures, the lower birth rate in European republics since 1940 has a great deal to do with the low rate of European working-age population growth. (TsSU, Vol. 2, 1972: 12-15)

Meeting their labor force needs places the Soviets on the horns of a dilemma similar to that faced in 1944. Increasing fertility is essential to future labor force needs, but meeting current demands for labor necessitates the employment of women. And, as we have seen, female employment is closely associated with low fertility. The problem, as before, is how to reconcile these two conflicting needs. Family policy to date has failed to substantially aid women in combining the mother-worker roles.

As a consequence of their predicament, some Soviet experts are opting for a lessening of female employment in an effort to increase the birth rate. (Cf. Laptenok and Rubin, 1971; Larmin, 1972: 15) The alarm about high female employment is real enough. Cohn (1973: 49) warns that ". . . if as high a percentage of women as works today continues to work in the productive sector, the labor shortage which is currently plaguing the USSR will reach crisis proportions in less than two decades."

On the other hand, current economic plans make female employment indispensible. According to Dodge (1966: 22), Soviet manpower needs are much greater than persons reaching working age can supply. An even higher participation of women seems to be the only recourse. Dodge's conclusions are supported by Cohn's (1973: 43) figures on Soviet employment. Presently over 92% of the Soviet working-age population is employed or in school, compared to 82% in 1959. Further labor force expansion will have to come from people now working private plots or from housewives. (Soviet dependence on private plots to supply foodstuffs makes the labor source from private plots unlikely. This leaves the housewife.)

The only other alternative to the Soviet dilemma is to greatly increase labor productivity and production, thus enabling women to leave the work force without any loss in the family's standard of living. (This is also suggested by Vermishev, 1973: 11) Increasing labor productivity would require the use of new technology, much of which comes from the capitalist West. And as we know from the recently aborted trade agreement between the USA and the USSR, the Soviets are wary of the political costs of too great a dependence on the West. Even if labor productivity could be greatly increased, at the same time growing consumer demands would also have to be met. Otherwise, improving productivity and output might simply add more fuel to the "consumer revolution" taking place. This in turn would further promote female employment and low fertility. So far the outlook for meeting consumption demands in the foreseeable future is not favorable. Soviet production at this time is not even capable of meeting the Five-Year Plan projections. The projected increase in consumer goods promised in the 1970-75 plan was reduced almost in half. (Cohn, 1973: 43)

One would have to conclude that, despite the gravity of the Soviet birth rate problem, it is not clear that the government is willing or able to make the economic investment necessary to promote childbearing at the desired level--especially without greatly reducing sorely needed female employment. Production of consumer goods and services has fallen below expectations, aid to families with children is not adequate to the need, and women still bear most of the domestic burdens in the home along with full time employment. These conditions make even a small family a tremendous burden in many cases.

In the 1970-75 Five-Year Plan, government efforts are indicated "for the purpose of creating better conditions for the upbringing of the younger generation." Nonetheless, as quoted by Vzhilianskii (1973: 53), the proposed package seems more a social welfare measure than a serious fertility incentive plan. The plan calls for

> . . . increased material assistance to families with children and the expansion of benefits to working mothers; the institution of child-support grants for families in which the average income per family member is less than 50 rubles a month; an increase in the number of paid days spent in caring for a sick child; the establishment of paid pregnancy and maternity leave equivalent to their full regular wage irrespective of time on the job; the expansion of the network of children's institutions.[34]

Undoubtedly, these proposals reflect government sensitivity to the problems of the family and are, in some cases, an expansion and improvement of 1944 family policies. Yet these measures, as was true of the 1944 policies, stand little chance of encouraging fertility to the point where the average family has the desired three children.

The most likely prospects are that, in the absence of more radical policies, fertility and labor force participation of women are going to remain much the same as now. Major changes are likely to be observed in rural and non-European areas where fertility and female employment have been less affected by forces of modernization. Once the impact of modernization is felt more strongly, rural and non-European groups should more closely resemble their urban neighbors, thus exacerbating the government's population problems.

FOOTNOTES

[1]Petersen (1975: 668-70) points out many defects in Soviet economic and demographic data, mostly prior to 1959. Petersen does note that there has been much improvement in recent years, although problems of reliability still exist.

[2]See Madison (1963).

[3]The following statement of Madame Kollontai, a major spokesman for sexual freedom and equality at this time, aptly defends the new ideological position on the family: "The old type of family has seen its day. . . . The family is ceasing to be a necessity of the State, as it was in the past; on the contrary, it is worse than useless, since it needlessly holds back the female worker from more productive and from more serious work." The quote is from Karel Hulicka, "Women and the Family in the USSR," Midwest Quarterly, 10 (January 1969), 133-53.

[4]Sul'kevich (1940), a Soviet demographer, boastfully compares the higher fertility levels and rate of growth of the Soviet population from 1926-39 with population trends in the West.

[5]See Coser (1951) who also points out that manpower needs were closely linked to the government's family policy.

[6]It is indicative of the Soviet pronatalist position that taxes after 1944 were levied on citizens with no children or less than three children. Citizens with no children paid 6% of their income; those with one child paid 1%; and those with two children paid 1/2%. Collective farmers, individual farmers and other farm personnel who paid agricultural taxes were assessed 150 rubles per year if they had no children. With one child they paid 50 rubles; with two they paid 25 rubles. Others with no children paid 90 rubles per year; with one child--30 rubles; and with 2 children--15 rubles. (Schlesinger, 1949: 372-73)

[7]Heer (1968: 234) also reveals that current payments are only .28% of the national income compared to, for instance, France's expenditure of 5% for family allowances.

[8]The cutbacks in the family allowance program, the encouragement for women to enter the labor force, and inadequate expenditures on housing are other reasons given to support the claim that the Soviets do not pursue a pronatalist policy.

[9]Improved aid to women in childbirth, financial support to large families, extension of creches and kindergartens, and tightening up on the criminal prosecution for nonpayment of alimony were also utilized by the government in 1936 to promote fertility. (Guins, 1954: 300)

[10]Passports are used for identification and internal movement in the USSR.

[11]Kurganov (1968: 143) argues that state payments were very inadequate compared to child support in previous legislation. In the old law the father paid 1/4 of his income for one illegitimate child, 1/3 for two. The state, under the new law, paid 5 rubles per month for one child, 7 rubles and 50 kopeks for two, and 10 rubles for three. Not only this but child support had been paid under the old law until the child reached 18; state payments ended after the child reached 12.

[12]Kurganov (1968: 204-08) believes that the scale of construction of new housing is exaggerated. For one, most apartments are only one- or two-room (in the USA, where fewer units are built, the number of rooms is usually about 5). Also the rapid increase in population due to migration vitiated much of the improvements in housing. Alex Nove (1969: 361-62) adds that due to agricultural failures that set back the rate of growth of the national income, the housing program was cut back after 1958.

[13]David and Vera Mace (1963: 156) recalled that during their trip to the USSR, the Russians were acutely embarrassed by their housing situation. "Seldom will they invite a Western visitor into their rooms. Even when you drive them home, they will always ask to be put down a block or two away so that you may not be able to identify the actual building in which they live."

[14]The relationship between female employment and fertility is well documented. In regard to postwar Europe see D. V. Glass, "Fertility Trends in Europe Since the Second World War." in S. F. Behrman et al. (eds.). Fertility and Family Planning. Ann Arbor: The University of Michigan Press, 1969.

[15]Soviet authors have isolated housing problems and the dual role of women--mother and worker--as important factors in marital discord. In 1965, according to Kurganov (1968: 192-93), of those getting a divorce in urban areas, 95% lived in unsatisfactory housing--one room in a communal apartment,

in a dormitory or with parents, etc. Only 5% of divorces involved people with separate apartments. And the best known Soviet family sociologist, A. G. Kharchev, and his associate, K. L. Emel'ianova, in "Brak: ideal i deistvitel'nost'," in G. V. Osipov et al. (eds.). Sotsial'nye issledovaniia, (Vypusk 4) Moskva: Nauka, 1970: 65, concluded the following from a study of married women in Leningrad: ". . . in half of the families, women have in fact a 'double work day'. . . . As a result many women age early, do not have time to look after themselves, waste their femininity and attractiveness, and become shrewish and irritable. In 37 families of 50 investigated quarrels and conflicts systematically occurred."

[16]Crude birth rates do not accurately measure the magnitude of the decline in urban fertility. During these five years, an enormous influx of young migrants to urban areas took place. This large number of young people would ordinarily tend to increase the crude birth rates, which are based on the number of births per 1000 total population.

[17]NEP--the New Economic Policy--ended in 1928 with the collectivization movement.

[18]The above figures include able-bodied workers only (men 16-59 and women 16-54). Wages are based on income in money and in kind. Income from pensions and private plots are excluded.

[19]In 1965 collective farmers began to receive some state-paid pension benefits, but the amount is far below that received by state employees. (Heer, 1968: 226-27)

[20]The life of the Russian rural woman has apparently retained much of its tsarist characteristics. A. S. Rappoport, in Home Life in Russia. New York: The Macmillan Company, 1913, 32-33, described the life of the peasant woman as one of hard work and little appreciation. Women worked constantly with little recreation. They had to work in the fields as well as doing all the housework. The husband never helped in the home. In fact, women were so little regarded in the peasant family that the birth of a girl could be a source of lamentation. "When the firstborn child is a girl, the friends of the family seize the father the day after the child's birth and throw him down and beat him."

[21]In discussing the 1944 family policies, E. Vorozheikin, in "Pravovoe regulir-ovanie otnoshenii braka is sem'i i narodonaselenie" pp. 34-51 in D. I. Valentei (ed.). Narodonaselenie. Moskva: Statistika, 1973: 37-38, expresses the view that awards, in concert with other incentives, are a good way to increase the birth rate.

[22]A few good references on demographic transition theory are as follows:
W. S. Thompson, "Population," American Journal of Sociology 34 (May 1929).
F. W. Notestein, "Population--the Long View" in T. W. Schultz (ed.). Food for the World. Chicago: University of Chicago Press, 1945. D. J. Bogue. Principles of Demography. New York: John Wiley and Sons, 1969.
K. Davis, "The Theory of Change and Response in Modern Demographic History" in T. R. Ford and G. F. Dejong (eds.). Social Demography. New Jersey: Prentice-Hall, Inc., 1970.

[23]See the following publications:
R. A. Easterlin, "Toward a Socio-Economic Theory of Fertility: A Survey of Recent Research on Economic Factors in American Fertility" in S. J. Behrman et al. (eds.). Fertility and Family Planning. Ann Arbor: University of Michigan Press, 1969.
W. Petersen. Population. New York: The Macmillan Company, 1969, 500-05.
G. Hawthorn. The Sociology of Fertility. London: Collier-Macmillan Limited, 1970.

[24]See D. J. Bogue. Principles of Demography. New York: John Wiley and Sons, Inc., 1969, 869-74, for a more detailed discussion of the GRR and NRR.

[25]Geographical disproportions in the sex ratio have also affected fertility to some extent, but the effect is local and not dealt with here. See V. A. Belova, "Analiz vliianiia no brachnost' semeinogo i vozrastno-polovogo sostava naseleniia" pp. 176-87 in A. G. Volkov, L. E. Dar'skii, and A. Ia. Kvasha (eds). Voprosy demografii. Moskva: Statistika, 1970.

[26]Size of family is based on the total number of persons living together related by kinship or a common budget. In 1970 of 58.7 million families, about 80% were married couples; and of these, over 3/4 had children. Of the 80% of married couples, 80% lived without relatives, 20% with relatives. About 4% of families were composed of two or more married couples. The remaining families (about 15%) were mothers or fathers with or without children or relatives. (TsSU, Vol. 7, 1974: 4-5)

[27]Heer in "Economic Development and Fertility" pp. 307-28 in William Petersen (ed.). Readings in Population. New York: The Macmillan Company, 1972: 312, uses the utility model and explains why the current development of non-European republics is not resulting in lower fertility, especially among those one would expect to reduce fertility; i.e., the better educated or those in higher occupational groups. Heer points out that such people have not yet developed a taste for the new consumption items available. Instead, they continue to "consume" more familiar items, such as children.

[28]A. K. (1969: 64) mentions that the high earnings in agriculture in Central Asia foster large families.

[29]See Schwarz (1948: 272-86).

[30]The slowdown is related to problems in the agricultural sector during this period. See Hanson (1968: 86-87).

[31]In an enlightening book on Soviet consumption, economist Margaret Miller (1965: 148-50, 157) notes that the Russian consumer who once eagerly bought whatever goods were available was beginning to reject goods on the basis of style and quality. The result was a most unusual Soviet government innovation--consumer market research. "The most popular demand is to under-take consumer research on an extensive scale. . . . Demand must be studied at all levels of the trade network and in the greatest possible detail, including such elements as fashion, colour, style, and probable future developments."

[32]There are data suggesting that the housing problem is not solved-- if utilities are considered. D. Valentei (1969: 56) gives 1966 figures on the availability of utilities in new apartments. In RSFSR--55% had running water, sewage, central heat, hot water, bath or shower. In the Central Economic Region the figure is 66%; in Western Siberia-- 58%; Eastern Siberia--51%; and in the Far East--only 14%.

[33]The transition in the Soviet view of population and family planning is disclosed in the following Soviet works (as well as many others): D. I. Valentei and E. Iu. Burnashev (eds.). Voprosy teorii i politiki narodo-naseleniia. Moskva: Izd. Moskovskogo Universiteta, 1970. Ia. N. Guzevatyi. Problemy narodonaseleniia stran Azii, Afrika i Laninskoi Ameriki. Moskva: Nauka, 1970. D. I. Valentei. Marksistsko-Leninskaia teoriia narodonaseleniia. Moskva: Izd. Mysl', 1971 and 1974.

[34]In November 1974, family allowances were extended to poor families in which average income per family member does not exceed 50 rubles per month. Each child is allowed 12 rubles per month up to his 8th birthday. (Larmin, 1974: 186)

BIBLIOGRAPHY

1969   Aitov, N. A.
"An Analysis of the Objective Prerequisites for Eliminating the
Distinction between the Working Class and the Peasantry" pp. 210-39
in G. V. Osipov (ed.). Town, Country and People. London:
Tavistock Publications.

1973   Altyeva, L.
"Rozhdaemost' v sel'skoi mestnosti Turkmenskoi SSR" pp. 71-82 in
D. I. Valentei (ed.). Narodonaselenie. Moskva: Statistika.

1971   Aper'ian, V. E.
"Demograficheskie faktory vosproizvodstva trudovykh resursov"
pp. 137-48 in D. L. Broner and I. G. Venetskii (eds.). Problemy
demografii, Moskva: Statistika.

1975   Belova, V. A.
Chislo detei v sem'e. Moskva: Statistika.

1972   Belova, V. A. and L. E. Dar'skii
Statistika mnenii v izuchenii rozhdaemosti. Moskva: Statistika.

1968
"Women's Opinions on Family Formation," Vestnik statistiki, No. 8,
2736.

1970   Berent, Jerzy
"Some Demographic Aspects of Female Employment in Eastern Europe
and the USSR," International Labor Review, 101 (Fall), 175-92.

1966   Bernard, Philippe J.
Planning in the Soviet Union. Paris: Pergamon Press.

1968   Boldyrev, V. A.
Ekonomicheskii zakon naseleniia pri sotsialisme. Moskva: Mysl'.

1970   Bondarskaia, G. A.
"Rol' Etnicheskogo Faktora v Formirovanii territorial'nykh razlichii
rozhdaemosti" pp. 160-75 in A. G. Volkov, L. E. Dar'skii, and
A. Ia. Kvasha (eds.). Voprosy demografii. Moskva: Statistika.

1968   Brackett, James W.
       "The Evolution of Marxist Theories of Population: Marxism Recognizes
       the Population Problem," Demography, 5, 158-73.

1963   Braverman, Harry
       The Future of Russia. New York: The Universal Library.

1971   Broner, D. L.
       "Sem'ia i zhilishchnye usloviia" pp. 149-60 in D. L. Broner and
       I. G. Venetskii (eds.). Problemy demografii. Moskva: Statistika.

1966
       Naselenie i narodnoe blagosostoianie. Moskva: Vysshaia shkola.

1968   Bronfenbrenner, Urie
       "The Changing Soviet Family" pp. 98-124 in Donald R. Brown (ed.).
       The Role and Status of Women in the Soviet Union. New York:
       Teachers College Press.

1971   Bronson, David W. and Constance B. Krueger
       "The Revolution in Soviet Farm Household Income, 1953-67" pp. 214-58
       in James R. Millar (ed.). The Soviet Rural Community. Chicago:
       University of Illinois Press.

1973   Cohn, Helen Desfosses
       "Population Policy in the USSR" Problems of Communism, 22 (July-
       August), 41-55.

1967   Cook, Robert
       "Soviet Population Theory from Marx to Kosygin" Population Bulletin,
       23 (October), 85-115.

1952
       "Soviet Population Policy" Population Bulletin, 8 (August), 17-27.

1951   Coser, Lewis
       "Some Aspects of Soviet Family Policy" American Journal of Sociology,
       56 (March), 424-37.

1947   Dallin, David J.
       The Real Soviet Russia. New Haven: Yale University Press.

1968   Dar'skii, L. E.
       "Tablitsy brachnosti zhenshchin SSSR (po vyborochnym dannym)"
       pp. 79-106 in A. G. Volkov (ed.). Izuchenie vosproizvodstva
       naseleniia. Moskva: Nauka.

1971   Dodge, Norton T.
"Recruitment and the Quality of the Soviet Agricultural Labor Force"
pp. 180-213 in James R. Millar (ed.). The Soviet Rural Community.
Chicago: University of Illinois Press.

1966
Women in the Soviet Economy. Baltimore: The Johns Hopkins Press.

1971   Dunn, Stephen P.
"Structure and Functions of the Soviet Rural Family" pp. 325-45 in
James R. Millar (ed.). The Soviet Rural Community. Chicago:
University of Illinois Press.

1968   Dzarasova, I. V.
"O zakone narodonaseleniia sotsialisma" pp. 37-46 in A. G. Volkov
(ed.). Izuchenie vosproizvodstva naseleniia. Moskva: Nauka.

1968   Eason, Warren E.
"Population Changes" pp. 203-40 in Allen Kassof (ed.). Prospects
for Soviet Society. New York: Praeger Publishers.

1968   Feldmesser, Robert A.
"Function and Ideology in Soviet Social Stratification" pp. 183-220
in Kurt London (ed.). The Soviet Union: A Half-Century of Communism.
Maryland: The Johns Hopkins Press.

1968   Geiger, H. Kent
The Family in Soviet Russia. Cambridge: Harvard University Press.

1960
"The Family and Social Change" pp. 447-59 in Cyril E. Black (ed.).
The Transformation of Russian Soviety. Cambridge: Harvard
University Press.

1954   Geiger, H. Kent and Alex Inkeles
"The Family in the USSR" Marriage and Family Living, 16 (November,
397-404.

1969   Gorkin, A.
"Concerns for the Soviet Family" Soviet Review, 10 (Fall), 47-53.

1954   Guins, George C.
Soviet Law and Soviet Society. The Hague: Martinus Nijhoff.

1970   Guzevatyi, Ia. N.
Problemy narodonaseleniia stran Azii, Afriki i Latinskoi Ameriki.
Moskva: Nauka.

1968
    "Aktual'nye problemy narodonaseleniia v Sovetskoi ekonomike" pp.
    9-22 in A. G. Volkov (ed.). Izuchenie vosproizvodstva naseleniia.
    Moskva: Nauka.

1968   Hanson, Philip
    The Consumer in the Soviet Economy. Evanston: Northwestern
    University Press.

1968   Heer, David
    "The Demographic Transition in the Russian Empire and the Soviet
    Union" Journal of Social History, 1 (Spring), 193-240.

1965
    "Abortion, Contraception and Population Policy in the Soviet Union"
    Demography, 2, 531-39.

1966   Heer, David and Judith G. Bryden
    "Family Allowances and Fertility in the Soviet Union" Soviet Studies,
    18 (October), 153-63.

1970   Iankova, Z. A.
    "O semeino'bytovykh roliakh rabotaiushchei zhenshchiny" pp. 76-87
    in G. V. Osipov, A. G. Kharchev, and Z. A. Iankova (eds.). Sotsial'nye
    issledovaniia. (Vypusk 4) Moskva: Nauka.

1968   Inkeles, Alex
    Social Change in Soviet Russia. New York: A Clarion Book.

1968   Inkeles, Alex and Raymond Bauer.
    The Soviet Citizen. New York: Atheneum.

1969   K., A. (sic)
    "A Demographic Problem: Female Employment and the Birth Rate"
    Problems of Economics, 12 (November), 61-68.

1971   Karcz, Jerzy F.
    "From Stalin to Brezhnev: Soviet Agricultural Policy in Historical
    Perspective" pp. 36-70 in James R. Millar (ed.). The Soviet Rural
    Community. Chicago: University of Illinois Press.

1969   Kharchev, A. G.
    "Leninizm i problema semeino-brachnykh otnoshenii" Nauchnye doklady
    vysshei shkoly, No. 5, 25-35.

1971   Kharchev, A. G. and C. I. Golod
    Professional'naia rabota zhenshchin i sem'ia. Leningrad: Nauka.

1968   Khorev, B. S.
        Gorodskie Poseleniia SSSR. Moskva: Mysl'.

1968   Kiseleva, G.
        "Vosproizvodstvo naseleniia i ego raionnye osobennosti" Voprosy
        ekonomiki, 8, 153-55.

1969   Kozlov, V. I.
        Dinamika chislennosti narodov. Moskva: Nauka.

1967   Kozyrev, Iu. N.
        "An All-Union Symposium on the Theory of Population" Vosrosy
        filosofii, 6, 140-44.

1948   Kulischer, Eugene M.
        Europe on the Move: War and Population Changes, 1917-47. New York:
        Columbia University Press.

1968   Kurganov, I. A.
        Zhenshchiny i kommunism. New York.

1967
        Sem'ia v SSSR. New York.

1974   Kvasha, I. Ia.
        "Ob usloviiakh uspeshnosti i otsenki effektivnosti demograficheskoi
        politiki" pp. 81-87 in V. S. Steshenko and V. P. Piskunov (eds.).
        Moskva: Statistika.

1974
        Problemy ekonomiko-demograficheskogo razvitiia SSSR. Moskva:
        Statistika.

1968
        "O nekotorykh instrumentakh demograficheskoi politiki" pp. 64-78
        in A. G. Volkov (ed.). Izuchenie vosproizvodstva naseleniia.
        Moskva: Nauka.

1971   Laptenok, S. and Ia. Rubin
        "The Family and the Production Activity of Women" Problems of
        Economics, 13 (February), 73-79.

1974   Larmin, O. V.
        Metodologicheskie problemy izucheniia narodonaseleniia. Moskva:
        Statistika.

1972
"On General and Specific Laws of Population" Problems of Economics, 15 (June), 3-23.

1953   Lorimer, Frank
"The Nature of Soviet Population and Vital Statistics" The American Statistician, 7 (April-May), 13-18.

1963   Mace, David and Vera
The Soviet Family. Garden City, N.Y.: Doubleday and Company, Inc.

1963   Madison, Bernice
"Russia's Illegitimate Children Before and After the Revolution" Slavic Review, 22 (March), 82-95.

1944   Maurer, Rose
"Recent Trends in the Soviet Family" American Sociological Review, 9 (1944), 242-49.

1973   Mazur, D. Peter
"Fertility and Economic Dependency of Soviet Women" Demography, 10 (February), 37-51.

1968
"Birth Control and Regional Differentials in the Soviet Union" Population Studies, 22, 319-33.

1967A
"Reconstruction of Fertility Trends in the USSR" Population Studies, 21 (July), 33-52.

1967B
"Fertility among Ethnic Groups in the USSR" Demography, 4, 172-95.

1966   Mehlan, K. H.
"The Socialist Countries of Europe" pp. 207-26 in Bernard Berelson et al. (eds.). Family Planning and Population Programs. Chicago: University of Chicago Press.

1971   Merkov, A. M.
"Demograficheskie issledovaniia v sotsial'noi gigiene" pp. 161-68 in D. L. Broner and I. G. Venetskii (eds.). Problemy demografii. Moskva: Statistika.

1971   Millar, James R.
        "Themes and Counter-Themes in the Changing Rural Community" pp.
        ix-xv in James R. Millar (ed.). The Soviet Rural Community.
        Chicago: University of Illinois Press.

1965   Miller, Margaret
        Rise of the Russian Consumer. London: The Institute of Economic
        Affairs.

1969   Nove, Alec
        An Economic History of the U.S.S.R. London: The Penguin Press.

1970
        Novoe v zakonodatel'stve o brake i sem'e. Moskva: Iuridicheskaia
        Literatura.

1970   Osborn, Robert J.
        Soviet Social Policies: Welfare, Equality, and Community. Homewood,
        Ill.: The Dorsey Press.

1966   Ovcharov, V. K.
        "Rozhdaemost' i perspectivy rosta naseleniia" Sovetskoi
        zdravookhranenie, 25, 54-57.

1969,   Petersen, William
1975   Population. New York: The Macmillan Company.

1964
        The Politics of Population. Garden City, N.Y.: Anchor Books.

1962   Pisarev, I. Iu.
        Narodonaselenie SSSR. Moskva: Sotsial'no-ekonomicheskoi literatury.

1968   Piskunov, V. P. and V. C. Steshenko
        "Vosproizvodstvo gorodskogo naseleniia Ukrainskoi SSR" pp. 225-44
        in A. G. Volkov (ed.). Izuchenie vosproizvodstva naseleniia.
        Moskva: Nauka.

1974   Rosset, E.
        "Printsipy is problemy perskektivnoi politiki narodonaseleniia" pp.
        52068 in V. S. Steshenko and V. P. Piskunov (eds.). Demograficheskaia
        politika. Moskva: Statistika.

1967   Riasentsev, V. A.
        Semeinoe provo. Moskva: Iuridicheskaia literatura.

1959 Roof, Michael M. and Frederick A. Leedy
      "Population Redistribution in the Soviet Union, 1939-1956"
      Geographical Review, 49 (April), 208-21.

1968 Sadvokasova, E. A.
      "Rol' aborta v osushchestvlenii soznatel' nogo materinstva v SSSR
      (po materialam vyborochnogo obsledovaniia)" pp. 207-24 in A. G.
      Volkov (ed.). Izuchenie vosproizvodstva naseleniia. Moskva:
      Nauka.

1963 Sauvy, Alfred
      Fertility and Survival. New York: Collier Books.

1944 Schlesinger, Rudolf (ed.)
      Changing Attitudes in Soviet Russia: The Family in the U.S.S.R.
      London: Routledge & Kegan Paul Limited.

1948 Schwarz, Solomon
      "The Living Standard of the Soviet Worker" Modern Review, 2
      (June), 272-86.

1969 Selivanov, V. I.
      "Primary Rural Collectives and their Social Functions" pp. 151-68
      in G. V. Osipov (ed.). Town, Country and People. London:
      Tavistock Publications.

1970 Sifman, R. I.
      "Dinamika plodovitosti kogort zhenshchin v SSSR (po dannym
      vyborochnogo obsledovaniia)" pp. 136-59 in A. G. Volkov, L. E.
      Dar'skii, and A. Ia. Kvasha (eds.). Voprosy demografii. Moskva:
      Statistika.

1968
      "Intervaly mezhdu rozhdeniiami i mezhdu vstupleniem v brak i
      pervym rozhdeniem" pp. 107-33 in A. G. Volkov (ed.). Izuchenie
      vosproizvodstva naseleniia. Moskva: Nauka.

1970 Smulevich, B. Ia.
      "Demografiia i politika" pp. 17-32 in A. G. Volkov, L. D. Dar'skii,
      and A. Ia. Kvasha (eds.). Voprosy demografii. Moskva: Statistika.

1970 Solov'ev, N.
      "Razvod, ego faktory, prichiny, povody" pp. 11-27 in A. Gyl'
      binskene et al. (eds.). Problemy byta, braka i sem'i. Vil'nius:
      Mintis.

1967   Somerville, John
        The Philosophy of Marxism. New York: Random House.

1974   Sonin, M. Ia.
        "O nekotorykh aspectakh izucheniia zakonomernostei dvizheniia
        naseleniia i demograficheskoi politiki" pp. 88-99 in V. S. Steshenko
        and V. P. Piskunov (eds.). Demograficheskaia politika. Moskva:
        Statistika.

1968   Sorlin, Pierre
        The Soviet People and Their Society. New York: Praeger
        Publishers.

1962   Sosnovy, Timothy
        "Town Planning and Housing" pp. 170-78 in Walter Laqueur and
        Leopold Labedz (eds.). The Future of Communist Society. New York:
        Frederick A. Praeger.

1968   Strumilin, Stanislav
        "Overpopulation Does Not Threaten Our Planet: a Soviet View"
        pp. 17-19 in Harry G. Shaffer and Jan S. Prybyla (eds.). From
        Underdevelopment to Affluence. New York: Appelton-Century-Crofts.

1940   Sul'kevich, S.
        Territoriia i naselenia SSSR. Moskva: Politizdat pri TsK VKP(b).

1950   Sverdlov, G. M.
        "Soviet Legislation on Marriage and the Family" Soviet Studies,
        2 (October), 192-201.

1972-74 Tsentral'noe Statisticheskoe Upravlenie pri Sovete Ministrov
         SSSR (TsSU) Itogi vsesoiuznoi perepisi naseleniia 1970 goda.
         Moskva: Statistika.
         Tom 1. Chislennost' naseleniia SSSR.
         Tom 2. Pol, vozrast i sostoianie v brake naseleniia SSSR.
         Tom 3. Uroven' obrazovaniia naseleniia SSSR.
         Tom 4. Natsional'nyi sostav naseleniia SSSR.
         Tom 5. Raspredelenie naseleniia SSSR po obshchestvennym gruppam,
                 istochnikam sredstv sushchestvovaniia i otrasliam
                 narodnogo khoziaistva.
         Tom 6. Raspredelenie naseleniia SSSR po zaniatiiam.
         Tom 7. Migratsiia naseleniia, chislo i sostav semei v SSSR.

1968
        SSSR v tsifrakh v 1967 gody. Moskva: Statistika.

1967   Strana sovetov za 50 let. Moskva: Statistika.

1963   Urlanis, B. Ts.
        Rozhdaemost' i prodolzhitel'nost' zhisni v SSSR. Moskva:
        Gosstatizdat.

1974,   Valentei, D. I.
1971   Marksistsko-Leninskaia teoriia narodonaseleniia. Moskva: Mysl'.

1969
        "Current Population Problems in the USSR" Problems of Economics,
        12 (November), 49-60.

1945   Venable, Vernon
        Human Nature: The Marxian View. New York: The World Publishing
        Company.

1973   Vermishev, K.
        "The Stimulation of Population Growth" Problems of Economics, 16
        (June), 3-13.

1973   (Vestnik statistiki)
        "Estestvennoe dvizhenie naseleniia, braki i razvodi v SSSR"
        No. 12, 73-89.

1973
        "Chislo i sostav semei" No. 11, 74-77.

1972
        "Zhenshchiny v SSSR, statisticheskie materialy" No. 1, 80-96.

1967
        "Pokazateli brachnosti i plodovitosti zhenshchin, statisticheskie
        materialy" No. 8, 87-95.

1972   Volkov, A. G.
        "Vliianie urbanizatsii no demograficheskie protsessy v SSSR"
        pp. 105-24 in Iu. L. Pivovarov (ed.). Problemy sovremennoi
        urbanizatsii. Moskva: Statistika.

1968
        "O nekotorykh prichinakh snizheniia koeffitsienta rozhdaemosti"
        pp. 171-83 in A. G. Volkov (ed.). Izuchenie vosproizvodstva
        naseleniia. Moskva: Nauka.

1971   Vucinich, Alexander
        "The Peasants as a Social Class" pp. 307-24 in James R. Millar
        (ed.). The Soviet Rural Community. Chicago: University of
        Illinois Press.

1973   Vzhilianskii, Iu.
        "Political and Economic Problems of Population under Socialism"
        Problems of Economics, 15 (April), 52-72.

1958   Wetter, Gustav
        Dialectical Materialism. New York: Frederick A. Praeger,
        Publisher.

1970   Zvidrin'sh, P. P.
        "Dinamika i demograficheskie faktory rozhdaemosti v Latvii" pp.
        236-56 in A. G. Volkov, L. E. Dar'skii, and A. Ia. Kvasha (eds.).
        Voprosy demografii. Moskva: Statistika.